In Love With Everything

Apophatic Mysticism

The Benefits and Dangers
of Love Without Reason

By Raymond Sigrist

Edited by Licia Rester and J. P. Jones

INFINITY
PUBLISHING.COM

ISBN 0-7414-5599-4

On the cover: the character for the Chinese word which is
pronounced "rong." In classical daoism, this character
means "the all-embracing."

Cover image design by Sheriann Ki Sun Burnham

If there is any profit obtained from the sale of this book, it
will be given to the International Children's Heart Foundation (babyheart.org) or to the Children's Shelter of Cebu
(cscshelter.org).

Published by:

INFIITY
PUBLISHING.COM

*1094 New DeHaven Street, Suite 100
West Conshohocken, PA 19428-2713
Info@buybooksontheweb.com
www.buybooksontheweb.com
Toll-free (877) BUY BOOK
Local Phone (610) 941-9999
Fax (610) 941-9959*

Printed in the United States of America

Published November 2009

Table of Contents

Acknowledgments

A thank-you to my two editors, Licia Rester and J. P. Jones, who have improved my manuscript to the extent that I might call them co-authors. I would like to thank Virginia Rester for giving me a translation of the *Dao De Jing* one day a long time ago. Another thank-you to Michael Saso for suggesting that I write this book and for sharing his knowledge of apophaticism. Scott Barnwell has been helpful for his insightful suggestions and his arguments with me as to my renditions of material from daoist texts. John Zodrow and Gina Rester-Zodrow provided valuable technical assistance and suggestions for changes in the manuscript. My appreciation to Elaina Eller and Mike Butler for editing previous writings on mysticism and my web page. Thanks to Gregg Miller who dragged me into the computer age.

I have learned whatever I know how to do from hundreds of people. The following is an alphabetized list of people each with whom I have spent many tens of hours discussing mysticism, daoism, and other closely related subjects.

Barbara Hamilton-Holway, Barbara Kristoff, Barry Childers, Bill Hamilton-Holway, Bill Slade, Camille Moser, Christina Zarkada, Darrell Connell, Dave Bagby, David Frazie, Doug Hollan, Eilan Loveridge, Gina Rester-Zodrow, Ginger Kuk, Gregg Miller, Norman Kuk, Hariputra das, Harrison John Adams, Igor Scerbo, Jan Brouwer, Jane Donnell, Jeffrey Ishmael, Joanne Carpenter, John Coscia, John Zodrow, Karen Baldwin, Ken Otter, Kerri

Brown, Kirk Ahrant, Laurie Anderson, Licia Rester, Linda Peltier, Louis Swaim, Luc Theler, Lynn Von der Werth, Lynne Sink, Margaret Holyoak, Marilyn Ericksen, Martha Black, Maria Martinez, Michaela McGivern, Mike Butler, Mike Carpenter, Mike Miller, Michael Sohigian, Nadine DeGuzman, Nina Correa, Nina Ruelas, Pat Murphy, Patti Vaught, Peter Haug, Ralph Cistaro, Rene Dean, Ruling Barragan-Yanez, Scott Ohrstom, Scott Railsback, Simona Fino, Sitara Lewis, Steven Jacobs, Taira Restar-Otter, Tammy Dyson, Terry Stiemsma, Tommy Baker, Tristen Haug, Wilma Fronda, Wong Yuen-Ming.

Author's Note

I remember waking up one day in the early '80s and feeling too heavy to get out of bed. As I stagnated for hours, I began to fantasize about ways I might escape existence, and I was particular about finding the right method. I am allergic to pain and have a deeply ingrained laziness, so I found myself looking for a method that would not cause too much pain, nor require too much work or inconvenience.

My desire for escape stemmed from having become bored with life. My religion and spiritual view of the world had stopped working for me several years earlier. And now I was also entirely bored with using a material approach to life. An overwhelming inertia enveloped me. It luckily was so intellectually and emotionally disabling that I became too inert to do anything further toward putting my thoughts of a painless and easy escape into an action plan. For a period of months I was able to survive and even go to work, but only by drinking eight to ten cups of coffee a day. This kept me going and animated me enough to largely prevent others from detecting my lethargic gloom. I don't like to share my problems; unlike other people, I find almost all of others' problems interesting, while my problems are of little interest to me.

I had become bored with life because in my mind I had completely figured out life and reduced it to a banal game. In the game I imagined that human life consisted of acting out the same six or seven patterns of human behavior. These same patterns recurred over and over again. Nothing new ever happened. For example, if you approached me with a pattern 6,

I would respond with pattern 3. If you did a 2, I would execute a 5. And so on. Anything that looked new and creative was actually only a cleverly hidden reproduction of one of the original small set of inevitable patterns. I had efficiently mapped out and created my own personal hell.

One day my friend Virginia Rester gave me a copy of the *Dao De Jing*, an ancient Chinese book credited to someone named Laozi. Laozi seemed to have found an uncannily creative way to escape the conventional patterns of human thought and interaction. I was initially impressed and soon became curious enough to look further to see whether I could apply his ideas to my own situation. If I could not escape hell, Laozi seemed to at least hold the promise that *an attempt* to escape might be interesting enough to keep me entertained for a long time.

And so I started down a path where I have found unexpected surprises. The path has not eliminated my alternating cycles of ecstasy and despair. But now each of these has become an experience of intense interest. Yes, even the despair. Although it is less frequent, it has become far too interesting to consider eliminating through self-destructive behaviors, either temporary or permanent. On the other hand, the periods of well-being have become deeper and more enduring. I am still following that path of Laozi today and continue to find it astonishingly entertaining at times.

I have discovered many things along this path, and this book will present some of my findings. One thing I discovered is that there is a learnable mystical know-how. I have learned how to do, and how not to do, a number of things. I have learned, for instance, that I can say something that is factually quite correct, and yet it can still be the stupidest thing to say when I have not listened carefully to what the other person was trying to tell me. Daily living has provided me with a number of opportunities to try out the mystical know-how. For example, I found out one night on the streets of Los Angeles that when a man points a gun at me, if I pay him the proper respect, I can give him my wallet but don't have to follow his demand that I next walk into the darkness behind my apartment building. In the town of Albany on a rainy night while massaging a dying woman as her daughter tearfully held her hand, I learned how there can be something unexpectedly right in a world where everything is turning out wrong. But, perhaps the most surprising thing I have learned is that we can develop a capacity to find wonder and satisfaction in any ordinary moment. Splendor is to be found everywhere just under the thin surface of a veil we call the mundane.

Now, here at the beginning of this book, I best initiate a candid relationship with you, my reader, that is, if I expect anything useful to come from this project. I have to confess to you, and not without a self-satisfying pride, that I would have started this book straightaway without giving you this small bit of my personal story, but my editors forced me to put it here. They tell me that other people are not interested in reading a writer who won't honestly share at least some small part of himself.

Raymond Sigrist
February 2009

Introduction

"Spirituality is the art of happiness for no reason."
Carla Ansantina[1]

Advisory for the mystical journey

The immediate world is too sudden and prolific. We pull back from it, recoil at the number of raw images spilling forth; we narrow our vision to shrink the awe of the totality that is here right now. We carefully ignore most of the astonishing phenomena constantly tumbling out of each moment. We must *think* our world in order to slow it down. To manage its unsettling impact, we carefully box it all up into neat concepts and ideas, and thus decrease its overwhelming intensity.

The mystic is less heedful. Eschewing the carefully groomed surface of her world, she plunges into the immediacy of it. She exposes her heart to the radiance of each unmediated moment. With the flood gates released, the exquisite splendor of the world pours in all at once, with all of its joy, poignancy, awe, and terror.

The slower I go, the faster I am carried. Slowness paradoxically expedites the mystical progression. There is nothing to be gained from haste. In fact, speed of success is directly correlated with patience and the acceptance of things as they now are. I suggest that this journey of the heart proceed prudently. There are times to pay heed and times when it is best to be thoughtlessly heedless; the voyage has opportunity for both disaster and great fortune.

We might describe mysticism as an uncannily responsive dynamic whose presence can become all-pervasive; a phenomenon by which we can continually establish harmony with whatever comes our way and, thereby, profoundly increase our enjoyment of life.

"Pragmatic apophatic mysticism" is the best description of my practice and the subject of this book, but in the interest of readability I will not carry on with that bulky term. I will simply call my subject "apophatic mysticism." By "pragmatic" I mean that I am simply looking for practical ways of enjoying my everyday life. I am not interested in finding a knowledge of what life "actually is"—my aim is not to realize some "true knowledge of life's fundamental meaning or purpose."

And so, please understand that I am speaking only of the pragmatic apophatic approach when I use the following more abbreviated terms: apophatic mysticism, mysticism, mystic, apophatic mystic.

My definition of apophatic mysticism follows Zhuangzi

I define apophatic mysticism as an uncanny state of psychic integration resulting from the suspension of all mental estimates of the source, identity, meaning, purpose, or value of the world of phenomena. As a result of this surrender of ideation and preconception, a surrender which is seldom if ever complete, one is able to transparently perceive and precisely respond to the compelling force and content of immediate experience. It is through this encounter with pure immediacy that one most fully engages the mystical dynamic.

My apophatic approach to mysticism follows in the tradition of the Chinese mystic Zhuangzi.[2] Most of the historical mystics who are considered to be apophaticists[3], like Zhuangzi, suspend what are known as <u>a priori</u> beliefs (preconceptions of what is true). But most other apophaticists, for example Muslim and Christian ones, have implicitly or explicitly assumed that human life certainly has some fundamental meaning. These religious apophaticists hold that this world we find around us has some fundamental purpose. And these other apophatic mystics assume that there are "ultimate concerns."

"How could I be certain of that?"
Zhuangzi, chapter 2[4]

Zhuangzi (or at least some of the authors who may have contributed to the book that bears his name) and other classical daoists closely associated with his thought stand apart from those who insist on the certainty that human life has a fundamental purpose and meaning.

Zhuangzi refrains from assuming that any characterization of our world of phenomena is absolutely true. He neither posits nor rejects any fundamental truth. His approach to evaluating the nature of the world is "wu chang," "not assuming anything to be eternally true." He does not assume there is any ultimate meaning or purpose of life. Nor does he deny that there is. Zhuangzi leaves open all questions that deal with fundamental truth, neither believing nor disbelieving. To differentiate him from other apophaticists who do believe in the certainty of an ultimate purpose for human life, we might call Zhuangzi's mysticism "pragmatic apophatic mysticism."

And please notice that I will be talking of *suspending* beliefs and disbeliefs. If I proposed eliminating any or all beliefs, I would merely be advocating another kind of belief.

No gods and no denial of gods

> "I have no reason to question your beliefs,
> I have no problem with them; the only ones
> that antagonize me are my own."
> Carla Ansantina

This book is about a mysticism which does not work if one insists on the existence of anything, and that includes gods or a God. It also will not work if one insists on believing that there are no gods or a God. Closely related to the issue of God and gods is the matter of ultimate concerns. This form of mysticism requires comprehensive open-heartedness and, therefore, the question of whether or not life has any ultimate meaning or concerns is left unanswered.

No guarantees of final happiness or anything else

> "To be completely free one needs to rigorously
> train oneself in a difficult skill: the ability
> to be wrong."
> Rawley Creed

Apophaticism implies giving up guarantees, for guarantees are incompatible with the openness apophaticism requires. As chapter two of *Zhuangzi* indicates, if I am unable to entertain the possibility that using my method might actually turn out to be a complete waste of my time, or even worse, then I have not grasped the basis of this method. To capture what we are aiming for, we have to let go of any guarantee that it will be found.

Putting words on it

"I don't know its actual identity,
And so I merely call it the way (dao).
If pushed to label it, I would call it mighty."
Laozi, chapter 25[5]

Mysticism is far too abstract and ambiguous to grasp with words. Let us not pretend we can present a definitive description of it. When for practical purposes I adopt an authoritative speaking or writing style, I hope both the reader and myself will realize we are pretending. Words may handily launch our journey but we will soon have to leave them far behind.

And so what is mysticism? Although I practice it, I frankly can't tell you exactly what it *is*; I suspect that the human mind cannot articulate it. If I am unable to claim to know anything for sure, what might I be able to do?

"Follow no set direction, have no set method,
then you can grasp the dao."
Zhuangzi, chapter 22

I can attempt to describe how mysticism works, and how it may affect your life. I can offer methods and suggest analogies that might clarify those methods. I can recommend practices that seem to have worked for me. I can suggest a tentative map to lead you to the *threshold* of the mystical experience. But I can't hand you the key that unlocks that door at the threshold. I can't specify the catalytic agent that produces a sudden flash of ecstasy occurring just beyond the threshold. No source outside of your own intuition will get you over the threshold and through that last door.

I can offer a provisional *operational* definition for mysticism, which is to say I can describe how it works.

First of all, we can start by thinking of mysticism as simply a dynamic force. It might be compared with gravity, an invisible and naturally occurring phenomenon which describes how a certain aspect of this world we live in operates and affects other phenomena.

The mystical dynamic, like gravity, is an invisible force which a person can either cooperate with, or oppose. We build a wall at a 90-degree angle to the surface of the earth because we want to cooperate with the force of gravity; the wall will be unstable if we alter this angle. As in the case of gravity, if we cooperate with the mystical dynamic, we can effectively apply its dynamic properties to enhance our lives. As Zhuangzi says, "You can grasp it even though you can not see it." (chapter 6)

> "The sage is happy with early death; also happy
> with an old age. He is happy with the beginning;
> and happy at the end."
> *Zhuangzi*, chapter 6

Mystics have discovered the principles of mysticism empirically, by direct experience. They have uncovered a secret that is difficult to believe: how to be content with everything just the way it is—and remain content no matter what else happens.

Is mysticism simply a description of another naturally occurring dynamic like gravity, or is it a manifestation of a supernatural force? The way mysticism is characterized (what one claims that it *really is*) varies among mystical traditions. For some it is simply a natural force; these might call it a sharp intensification of intuition. For others it is the manifestation of a personal God who can assure a believer's continued existence forever.

As to what mysticism "really is," this is a question about which the apophatic mystic continually remains ignorant. Ignorance of any fundamental truth forms the basis of Zhuangzi's mysticism. He was only interested in how it worked, not what it actually was.

"Yesterday Zhuang Zhou dreamed he was a butterfly and he so much enjoyed the butterfly's carefree winging about. He had apparently realized himself to be just what he wished and no longer recalled Zhou. Then suddenly he awoke again, and could see he was quite obviously Zhou. But now he could not really tell: was he Zhou who had dreamed he was a butterfly, or is it the butterfly who is now dreaming that he is Zhou? Zhou or the butterfly; there has to be some point where separate phenomena arise. It is this separating which is called the transformation of things."

Zhuangzi, chapter 2[6]

In the butterfly-dream story of the Zhuangzi, the author introduces us to the unusual way the daoist mystic assesses his experience; he is a person who cannot be certain what actually *is real*. Zhuangzi knows he had an unusual experience during the dream and its aftermath, but he finds that he cannot be sure just what "really happened." And he can't be sure what is still happening right now. Perhaps more surprising and significant, in chapter two of the *Zhuangzi* we find out that this *uncertainty is the very basis* of the apophatic mystic's *creative power*. The mystical ability depends on his not knowing for certain what anything really *is*.

"I rely on what I don't know."

Zhuangzi, chapter 30

The apophatic mystic does not care about what is *true*; she does not claim to know what is true. She is only concerned with what is mystically effective. Like

Zhuangzi, I do not claim to be describing either truth or reality. I attempt only to present what I hope will be useful characterizations of a subjective experience. My endeavor is to find out which characterizations of mystical experience might provide the most useful picture, that is to say, which ones may evoke mystical ecstasy.

Apophatic skill is based on trust in uncertainty

"Knowledge has that which it relies on for
its basis, but there is no reason to be certain
that any basis is reliable."
Zhuangzi, chapter 6

Optimal openness depends on uncertainty. Openness presents the author with a challenge. In order to maintain openness, one cannot be bound by any conclusive assumptions. For example, most writers at least implicitly assume that they occupy the same world as the reader. But as a writer taking an apophatic perspective, I cannot even assume that I live in the same world of experience as you. Anything I purport to be the case will be based on the world of my own experience; that world could significantly differ from yours.

"Optimal knowledge stops at what it does not
know."
Zhuangzi, chapter 23

In this book I am describing my own pragmatic apophatic path, and not necessarily the path of anyone else. If I would claim to know what is authentic for another person, I would be contradicting the very terms of apophaticism.

To simplify the text, I may at times write in a manner that appears to say or suggest that I am presenting a universally applicable concept. For example I might say something like "this is how it works." At such times, please remember that I do not claim any fundamental assumption that what I am putting forth must also be valid in your world.

> "My religion is apophatic. This means that
> I believe your religion might quite possibly
> be the true religion."
> Rawley Creed

My primary interest is intimately connecting with my world and, therefore, with you, my reader. I will do that best by not deeming my experience to reflect "the exclusive truth." We will communicate better if I don't try to fit you into a slot within my "normative" world. Perhaps we live in the same world. Or perhaps we live in two truly different worlds, and by sharing our impressions we each can expand our own "true" world.

Ups and downs

Most religious and spiritual traditions explicitly state or implicitly suggest that if you follow their teachings long enough and well enough you will finally reach a perfected state of being. You will be ultimately "delivered." Apophaticism offers no such promise.

My own spiritual path is a continuing journey of ups and downs. Some of the lows have been exquisitely painful and, at the same time, quite useful. During each low period, I am able to discover and attain skills which I can fruitfully apply during the next high, and also during the next low. The next high phase is usually more interesting, more enjoyable, steadier, and longer lasting than the previous one. The next low is usually less vexing than the last.

If, and only if, I am able to skillfully process a period of gloom, then the more depressing it is, the better. I can benefit the most from what I learn at the very bottom, if I am able to survive the bottom.

I do not seek a "final attainment." I do not expect to reach a complete, unending sense of perfection. I look forward to an interminable journey of discovery and wonder. I have found an unreasonable love for this world just as it is, richly unfolding in each newly arrived moment, bearing treasures whether the moment brings joy or gloom.

The apophatic disclaimer

> "Anyone who is completely convinced
> of the value of apophatic mysticism is not
> qualified to write a book about it."
> Rawley Creed

Apophaticism has implicit disclaimers. For example, in this book I hope to present some useful insights on mysticism. But looking from the apophatic perspective, there is no warrant for me to claim that you will find any material here whose validity transcends my own subjective experience. It would be presumptuous to claim that the material is more reliable than that drawn from any other kind of subjective experience. Ironically, a would-be apophaticist who claimed to present anything more than his own subjective experience would be one who had lost the very basis of apophaticism.

There is also no justification for categorically guaranteeing that the reader will benefit from the practices described herein. The least prudent thing I could do would be to unequivocally advocate the apophatic practice.

Certainty about anything is difficult to justify, and it nearly always causes a trip up when applied to the dynamically changing landscape of mysticism. The creative efficacy of apophatic mysticism depends on having an unstable ground.

The book is not meant for everybody. It is primarily aimed at those of you who, like me, have what might be considered an unhealthy obsession; you yearn to eliminate everything that comes between you and the unspeakable grip of the mystical experience.

You are folks who recognize that in practicing mysticism you are *not* a member of a noble spiritual elite. You suspect that the temptation to believe your endeavors are superior to, or less self-indulgent than, those of any other being is a farce. You understand that if you are convinced that your path is one of a higher nobility, this will prevent you from approaching the astonishing treasure you so dearly seek.

Mystical ecstasy

This book is about a tool, not a creed. This tool can be used in the attainment of mystical ecstasy—that singular experience which is at once both the mother and child of unconditional love.

The apophaticist's intention is to continually realize this ecstasy, the nearly unshakable sense of well-being which is sometimes called "non-contingency" or "deliverance." Non-contingency means that the mystic's ecstatic realization has freed her sense of well-being from the impingement of material events. Whether she loses a book or a foot, she will be able to readily recover her happiness. Although things might happen which cause her a period of sadness, no matter what happens, she will not lose the profound sense of well-being which resides at the center of her being.

A mysticism of *self-interest*?

In this book I present my own mystical practice, a practice similar to the apophatic mysticism described in the *Zhuangzi* and other "classical daoist" books, works written more than 2000 years ago in China. The *Zhuangzi's* authors are notable for candidly admitting that the aim of their practice is *self-serving*; they desired sovereign contentment. Their writings tell of the mystical adept's empirical discovery of this treasure. The adept attains it by developing a keen interest in the subtle dynamics of her perceptual field. This field contains a world of phenomena which, for better and worse, includes other beings and their sometimes opposing interests.

The mystic soon finds out that it is in her best self-interest to "get outside of her self" and become exquisitely interested in the motivations, desires, and concerns of these other beings. It is only out here with you others that she will be able to realize unreasonable love and unspeakable joy. Stepping outside of herself serves her well.

Notes:

1. Who are Carla Ansantina and Rawley Creed? They are voices I hear at times, often in the middle of the night, voices who are less modest and more certain of things than I would dare to be. Carla and Rawley are more heretical, and yet they also seem more dogmatic toward their heresies, than I would think proper. I am not comfortable with their candor; their thoughts are troublesome and thus potentially transporting for me. Rather annoyingly, Carla and

Rawley can contradict themselves and don't have to explain. I wish I had that license.

2. I am following Michael A. Sells and Harold D. Roth in applying the term "apophatic" well beyond the scope of Christian mysticism and especially following Roth, to the writings and concepts of Zhuangzi and the other classical Chinese daoists.

See Michael Sells: *Mystical Languages of Unsaying*, Michael A. Sells, The University of Chicago Press, 1994, page 4.

See Harold Roth: "Early Daoist Mystical Praxis" in *Religious and Philosophical Aspects of the Laozi*, Edited by Mark Csikszentmihalyi and Phillip J. Ivanhoe (Albany: The State University of New York Press, 1999) page 89; note 14.

For simplification I will later use the name "Zhuangzi" as if there were one person named Zhuangzi who wrote the book bearing this name. Scholars believe there were at least several authors of the book. The same holds true for the other ancient Chinese texts of the daoists.

3. As Michael Sells says (see above note), the application of the term "apophaticism" to mysticism dates from the Greek writer Plotinus (died in 270 C.E.). Christian apophaticists later used the term to indicate a practice during which all conceptual ideas of God are suspended in order to obtain a direct experience of God. In contrast to the Christian apophaticists, my use of the more nuanced term "pragmatic apophaticism" indicates only that a remarkable mystical experience is obtained through the suspension of conceptual thought, but what the cause of that experience is remains open to question. One might say that the Christian apophaticist empties her heart so that she may experience God,

while the pragmatic apophatic empties her heart so that she may experience the "whatever it is."

4. In this book I will quote from a number of Chinese daoist texts: *The Laozi, The Zhuangzi, The Guanzi, The Liezi,* and *The Huainanzi.* The texts are named after their purported authors, but no one knows if any persons bearing these names ever existed.

5. The English interpretation of the Chinese from the daoist texts which I cite is my own. I am not a trained translator of Chinese and so I would call my renderings "interpretations," rather than translations. My concern is not so much that my renderings are completely true to the intentions of the texts, but rather whether or not my renderings are performative: do they instigate the performance of apophatic praxis? The copies of text in Chinese script which I have used in this book come from a collection of citations from Chinese texts which I have collected for many years. I more recently compared these collected citations against those of Donald Sturgeon's "Chinese Text Project" (http://chinese.dsturgeon.net), and I have generally used his selections of Chinese text where it differed from my much less well-researched collection.

6. Zhuangzi is making a point here which is similar to today's postmodernist interpreters. The author, let alone the reader, cannot ascertain whether or not what he is reporting is truly an accurate interpretation of his own experience.

Part One

Speaking of the unspeakable.

1

How I am using these words

Please note that the following definitions indicate how *I* am using these terms, and not what these words might mean to others.

Mystical disposition

I will often use this term instead of the more common identifiers such as the *mystical experience* or *mystical state*. I take this mystical disposition to be a particular dynamic arrangement of the psyche. In this disposition the various components of the psyche are interacting in an uncanny manner which results in the mystical phenomenon called *liberation, non-contingent contentment,* or *mystical ecstasy.*

Spirituality

I use the term spirituality to mean an intuitively directed process of communication and collaboration transpiring between the individual's natural desire to express her vitality and the other forces within the world which she inhabits. It describes the relationship between a nexus of awareness (sometimes called *me*) and the field of perception around that nexus (sometimes called *my world*).

Psyche

When I use the terms *psyche* and *psychic,* I am referring to the individual's total body and mind sensory-responsive communication system; I am not referring to anything in the realm of para-psychology, such as psychic phenomena. The psyche is a dynamic system of perception, integration, and generation of responses to the continually changing data of perception. I am using the term to indicate a process; I am not describing a fixed entity with an independent existence.

Fundamental value versus practical value

What is the difference between fundamental value and practical value? Fundamental value indicates the basic immutable faultlessness that is sensed by the mystic to be intrinsic to every being. Practical value indicates a measure of value something has with regard to a specific limited use of it. For example, a ball is practically useful for bouncing, a brick is not. Harming another being in a manner that is considered to be wrong by one's community makes the assailant have less practical value in her community. And on the other hand, the mystic does not see such a person as having any less fundamental value; that person, like every other being, is felt to be essentially faultless.

Deliverance

Deliverance in apophatic mysticism is deliverance to the immediacy of ecstasy. I don't take this to necessarily be deliverance to a God, nor to an absolute, nor to "the end of all suffering." I don't take apophatic deliverance to be a deliverance from human mortality; I don't necessarily see it as a final solution to human angst. All of these final notions of deliverance, in my experience, interfere with the optimization of apophatic deliverance. The apophatic is simply a deliverance of naked psychic awareness to the fullness of the moment. Rather than finalize anything, apophaticism optimally reduces the human's natural dissatisfaction with the fact that these apparently unsolvable problems exist.

Deliverance includes the realization of universal faultlessness, or "okayness." The mystic senses that she and every other being are fundamentally acceptable just the way they are. She realizes a sense that nothing any being has every done, or is doing, can decrease their immutable worth.

Rapture

I distinguish between what I call *ecstasy* and what I call *rapture*. I characterize rapture as an acute emotional and visceral sense of euphoria, an experience with an intensity of feeling comparable to that of sexual orgasm. In contrast, an experience of mystical ecstasy as I define it has various levels of emotional intensity and produces a more continuous sense of well-being than rapture. I discuss mystical ecstasy in further detail in chapter 11.

Compelling

I use the word *compelling* to describe my emotional experience of the mystical ecstasy. I don't call it an experience of God or an experience of the Absolute because, like Zhuangzi, I don't claim to know the true characterization/identity of my experiences. I only know what various experiences feel like. Some are compelling and some are not.

A sense of

Closely related to *compelling* is *a sense of. A sense of* merely reports an experience; it posits no ontological status. Thus I will say the apophaticist has a sense of unity with everything, rather than "he realizes that he is identical with everything."

Optimal

This word is used instead of the word perfect which appears so often in spiritual literature. There is no apparent justification for claiming anything to be perfect, whatever that perfection might mean. And perfection gives an additionally unjustified suggestion that all of the existential problems of the human being can be solved. Mysticism lets me enjoy life despite a number of apparently unbeatable challenges to that enjoyment.

Whatever it is

I use this term as shorthand for *whatever it is that is operating at this moment* to cause mystical ecstasy. The mystic trusts in the *whatever it is* because so far it has brought her much benefit. I also use the word *jewel* as a metaphor for *whatever it is*.

Void versus nullity

The term *nullity* implies that all experience is worthless and all existence is worthless—that is to say all phenomena are *null*. On the other hand, the mystical *void* represents the psycho-spiritual disposition that is open to all possibilities, open to the idea of value and meaning, but also open to the possibility of nullity. In the void the mystic does not rule nullity in or rule it out.

Field of perception

I generally speak of "the mystic and his relationship with his field of perception," rather than saying, "the mystic and his relationship with the world." In this way, I am keeping to the mystic's report of his experience, rather than assuming that his experience is part of a greater reality (or that an ultimate reality even exists).

Spiritual poverty

Spiritual poverty refers to the action of assuming nothing. In this way, I meet the moment on its own terms. I am ready for anything and everything to be different from what I had supposed it would be. I surrender my expectations to the jewel, that is to say, to the dynamics of mysticism, even though I am aware that I might be surrendering to a self-deception. That possibility does not matter to me; I surrender simply because the surrender delivers what I want. With a great reduction of expectations, including a great lessening of hope and of hopelessness, I am able to realize and enjoy the astonishing quality and sufficiency of the emerging moment.

Higher and lower values

In referring to mysticism, I try to avoid using words such as *higher*, which suggests that mystical praxis is an intrinsically more worthy endeavor than, for example, drinking beer. Instead of a *higher* form of awareness, I take mystical awareness to be a *wider* and more *comprehensive* form of awareness. Practically speaking, it can *see more*. It is an awareness which allows for the possibility that anything might be intrinsically more or less noble than anything else; it permits the possibility that all formulations which posit fundamental values might be void of meaning. If I believe my efforts are nobler than another man's effort to drink more beer or eat more hotdogs, I am not practicing apophatic mysticism.

2

An apophatic formula

There are a number of deceptively simple mystical formulas which describe apophatic cultivation and practice. In actual practice the mystical process involves a complex feedback system; all stages of the process feed back to and reinitiate changes in the other stages. Here, I'll give an example of one process schematically presented in linear form.

A basic apophatic schematic is presented in *Laozi*, chapter 45:

清靜為天下正

Phonetically this is "Qing jing wei tianxia zheng." It can be translated as: "Through clarity and equanimity everything (spontaneously) falls into place."

The formula indicates that when one clearly senses everything in one's field of perception and is able to maintain an attitude of equanimity towards all this data, events will spontaneously unfold and culminate auspiciously.

清 Qing: Clarification

Let's look at the Laozi formula step by step, starting with clarification (qing).

To move toward mystical ecstasy, the first priority is attaining clarity. To achieve a clear and open view, one must eliminate anything which is preventing a lucid vision of the entire perceptual field. Preconceptions are the main obstructions to this field. We tend to see only what we expect or want to see, filtering out whatever does not fit our previous assumptions.

The mystic clears the perceptual field of such filters; he removes the limits placed upon it by dogmatically held preconceptions. Provisional preconceptions are not a problem. For example, I can provisionally assume I will burn my hand if I place it too close to a flame. My mystical vision will be hindered only if I become absolutely convinced of the exact point at which it will be burned by that flame; indeed mystical vision fails me whenever I am absolutely sure of anything.

The apophatic disposition requires a provisional suspension of any belief in absolutes, whether scientific or religious. On this path one avoids these absolutes, not because one can be certain of the impossibility of absolutes, but because harboring perceived absolutes within the mind has been found empirically to limit a clear open vision. Radical openness is necessary to experience the profoundly mystical.

Although the apophaticist remains uncertain of all claims, to survive he will need to draw provisional conclusions about his world. In order to leave his house, he will tentatively assume that going out by the door will be better than exiting by an upstairs window. But like all of his other assumptions, this one remains provisional. The field of perceptual data is quite changeable. Something unexpected might happen that makes the window a better exit than the door.

Clarification especially includes seeing what is clearly not needed, seeing those things which are harbored in the mind and which are counterproductive to a desired outcome. For example, I best not

as if by magic. But this is not wizardry; the connections are always there but normally overlooked. By resting in clarity and inner stillness, I remove those distractions which have taken my attention away from the remarkable interplay which is occurring in the world around and within me. With enhanced perception I notice a multitude of opportunities and exploit the collaborative power drawn from auspicious coincidences.

為天下 **Wei tianxia: Cause things to**

Wei in Chinese means to cause or to consummate. *Tianxia* is literally *everything under heaven*. In our formula (Qing jing wei tianxia zheng), *tianxia* refers to all of the beings and affairs which the mystic encounters each moment. He has an unusual knack for moving individuals to more effectively act in their own self-interest, and most interestingly it is merely his clear and tranquil presence which causes the changed behavior. For example, I see the way the mystic is looking at me and I recognize what that uncanny look is pointing out; from what I see in him, I understand that I can do what I need to do.

The mystic has made no prior plan or agenda for what he might like to happen; what happens in his presence will be largely unpredictable. Few if any words are spoken by him, and yet those within his gaze feel they are understood and their aspirations valued by him. Freed to sense their own inherent power, they are moved to effectively serve themselves.

正 **Zheng: Reach optimal potential**

Zheng indicates the reaching of optimal potential. The adept's mystical resonance with his world by itself propels the individuals and affairs around him to reach higher potentials. He makes this happen by intuitively setting in motion a subtle interplay among all those in his vicinity. He has catalyzed the initiation of a synergetic feedback system. In this system the various players are consciously or unconsciously moved to join a beneficial collaborative effort. While each may be focused on their own benefit, they will also unknowingly benefit all others who are present. Among those present there may even be some who are enemies of others.

> "I decree nothing and the people correct themselves."
>
> *Laozi*, chapter 57

Periodically I've gotten reports like the following one from a teenage girl:

> "One time on a bus I sat suffering and confused about what to do next in my life. A woman got on a few stops past Arcadia Street and sat down next to me, introducing herself as Sara. Before I knew what was happening, I was practically telling this stranger my whole life story. Sara gave me no advice and in fact hardly said a thing but I could tell she was catching every word and everything in between my words. My monologue went only about twenty minutes, but when we said good-bye I was quite clear about what I needed to do next. Strangely enough I felt eager to face the difficult decisions I now planned to make. Sara had somehow let me understand I could do whatever I had to do, and without needing someone else to tell me how to do it."

The mystic's power is neither directive nor sovereign; it is catalytic and collaborative. He cannot make people do what he wants, but he can move them to discover and obtain what is in their own benefit. He gives little if any advice; his skill is creating an environment conducive for the other person to autonomously change and reach her optimal potential.

3

Unspeakable terror

For effective mystical praxis, it is useful to put a discussion of mysticism in a context which includes both the wonders and the horrors of our world. It is worth taking more than a moment to reflect on the great suffering that is continually going on around us. For example during part of the time period in which I am writing this book, there have been tens of thousands of people killed from a typhoon in Burma and from an earthquake in China.

For better and worse, during my life I have directly watched the occurrence of unspeakable horror in various times and places. I've observed it on a number of occasions at the moment in which it occurred. At times terror has been something I heard happening at a distance of several miles away, and at other times it's been a few feet away looking me in the face.

I don't know what the meaning of this kind of horror is. I don't know what, if any, authentic role terror might play in this world. Is there a reason for it to exist? The truth is that as I have cured my desire to discover what the existence of the world itself might mean, I have also ended my desire to find a rational meaning for its terror. These days I am only interested in having this world work well for me. It works much better for me if I don't try to explain away its terror.

It is rather unhandy for me at times, but it turns out that this world serves me better if I take a sincere and avid interest in listening to what you say the beauty and terror of this world mean to you. If you tell me the world holds unreasonable terror for you, I will be able to accurately hear what you are saying as long as I don't try to convince you or myself that there must be some logical scheme which makes sense of terror.

4

Openness and surrender

When Bodhidharma met Emperor Wu of the Liang dynasty, the Emperor asked: "What is the Holiest ultimate truth?" The Bodhidharma answered: "Openness. Hold nothing Holy!"[1]

The mystical disposition which the apophaticist seeks requires that nothing is permanently (dogmatically) stored in his mind. Such heavily weighted data could easily obscure his view of the contents of this moment, which is continually unfolding, bearing its intricately interacting contents.

An example of a mind holding on to something with too much weight would be a mind which has the notion of something being *holy*. This is what was expressed in that ironic exchange between Bodhidharma and Emperor Wu.

"Apply emptiness to the optimal degree."
Laozi, chapter 16

If I have consciously or unconsciously precluded the possible occurrence or the absence of any phenomenon, I have restricted the scope of my awareness, and will be inhibited in attaining a comprehensive view of my perceptual field. To hold this moment open, I must be free to imagine anything. If there is something I cannot suppose, and that thing, or something similar, shows up, I will very likely not see it.

There are two aspects to the endeavor of maintaining open psychic receptivity. The first is limiting one's mind to a sharply reduced collection of preconceptions, data consisting of both mundane and metaphysical dogma. With the mind having as few fixed preconceptions as feasible, one can better perceive and integrate new data. The second is reducing ongoing discursive thinking. This reduction in cognitive processing increases the psychic space for the deeper and more powerful intuitive processes to function.

By employing open awareness, the mystic is able to effectively perceive, integrate, and respond to all the data contained in this moment. If his beliefs or disbeliefs are censoring the reception of any relevant data, he will not be effective. The effective processing of everything contained in this moment gives rise to mystical ecstasy.

吾惡乎知之?

"How would I know that?"
Zhuangzi, chapter 2

Zhuangzi's point here is that he suspects he is unable to conclude anything with certainty. This very lack of certainty forms the basis of effective mystical awareness. It is an open awareness where almost no possibility is ruled out or ruled in, *ahead of time*. The *time* in question is this moment of immediate awareness—right here, right now.

Zhuangzi enters the next moment without any certainty regarding what might happen. He expects he might even find that everything he thought to be the case will turn out to be incorrect. This gives him the ability, as he puts it, "to make a springtime with everything."

Let's compare Zhuangzi's approach with that of a Christian mystic to highlight the radical nature of the daoist's surrender to uncertainty. The Christian empties her mind of concepts so she can engage her God. She is certain beyond doubt that during this mystical engagement she has directly experienced the creator of the universe.

"If you, nevertheless, ask how it is possible that the soul can see and understand that she has been in God, since during the union she has neither sight nor understanding, I reply that she does not see it then, but that she sees it clearly later, after she has returned to herself, not by any vision, but by a certitude which abides with her and which God alone can give her."[2]

Saint Teresa

In contrast to Teresa's admirable certainty, the method of the classical daoist is to empty the mind of certainty and open it up to any possibility. His aim is to enjoy life without regard to whether or not fundamental truths about life can be ultimately relied upon.

More specifically, he suspends any judgment as to whether or not his own ideas reflect any fundamental truth. Furthermore, he has no idea how long his suspension of this judgment will prove to be beneficial. Zhuangzi's term for this is *hengfu*. Hengfu means making an interminable surrender of a claim to know the final truth of, or value of, any phenomenon. Ironically, and important to daoist praxis, this means he would not be certain that Saint Teresa could not be certain.

"Don't impoverish your mystical ability by what you think you know."

Zhuangzi, chapter 16

To maintain the openness necessary for the practice of pragmatic apophaticism, the mystic cannot assert that there is a God, nor can he assert there is not one. Pragmatic mysticism requires he provisionally surrender all fixed beliefs and all fixed disbeliefs. To be open, he can be neither a believer nor an atheist. Nor can he claim that either of those advocates are mistaken in their beliefs.

> "Claiming something can be described as only being 'this way' will have a certain degree of correctness to it, and also a certain degree of incorrectness."
>
> *Zhuangzi*, chapter 2

Zhuangzi tells us that mystical know-how does not rely on knowing whether any purported fact is true or not. Mystical know-how depends on surrendering my death grip on what I think is true, and then following an intuitive path with a minimal amount of anticipation of where I think it might be taking me.

Zhuangzi is telling us that we will need to acquire a particular know-how to practice mysticism, but we will grasp this ability only by giving up our need to know whether it or anything else is eternally reliable or not. I best surrender any assurance that this know-how will always continue to serve my best interests.

There is a wonderful utility in using the term *pragmatic* when contrasting this type of apophatic mysticism with that of other apophaticists. The word pragmatic suggests the mystic is not claiming his actions are fundamentally noble ("noble" as contrasted with "ignoble"). Instead, he is simply attempting to get something he wants. In most mystical traditions, the idea of wanting something for oneself is considered to be an unseemly motivation. In contrast, the pragmatic apophaticist is careful not to immodestly claim that he is free of such self-serving motivations!

"Paradoxically, stripping away illusions
especially includes getting rid of the idea
that I can ever be certain that I am not
deceiving myself."
Rawley Creed

Openness is the means of mystical progression; it involves the suspension of all conceptual anchors and fundamental evaluations. This suspension is often disconcertingly destabilizing, but it allows the mystic to proceed pragmatically, empirically, intuitively, and effectively. If a particular conception, method, or value is found to work well, it is used until it no longer works, or no longer is needed.

Openness often entails the destruction of some dearly held beliefs. It turns out that the more emotionally distressing the destruction of an idea is, the more its potential to be wrought into a vehicle of mystical deliverance. Of particular benefit is the distress undergone when the mystic sees his own folly in making a particular spiritual assumption.

Profound self-doubt is the most expedient doorway to mystical deliverance.

"The purpose of the trap is the fish.
When the fish is caught, forget about the trap."
Zhuangzi, chapter 26

What I hold in my mind determines the quality of my responsiveness. Concepts stored in the mind continually arise and affect, often negatively, the ability of consciousness to receive and integrate new perceptual data. The adept minimizes his habit of making cognitive conclusions and getting attached to conceptual views so that his scope of perception and flexibility of responsiveness may be optimally unrestricted.

The greatest value of openness is that it increases the mystic's ability to be in intimate communication with other beings. Personally, this is the most enjoyable activity I have yet found. I find the degree of intimacy I can attain with you (the other) is directly dependent on the extent to which I am able to encourage you to generate your own autonomous perspectives and systems of value independent of my opinions and prejudices. My openness to the value of your uniquely different point of view greatly increases the treasures awaiting me in this moment.

Notes:

1. My translation, from the Chan *Blue Cliff Record*.

2. James, William. *The Varieties of Religious Experience*. (New York: Random House, 1929), p. 400.

5

Self-deception

Once, I read a book called *The Catcher in the Rye* by J. D. Salinger. I laughed at the way the young protagonist Holden made fun of snobs. But later I was mortified as I realized that his and my own making fun of snobs is quite snobbish behavior.

Self-deception as a possibility is useful to consider at both the practical and philosophical levels. It is useful to realize I can never be guaranteed of eliminating all self-deception. In fact I might be entirely mistaken about nearly everything. I can only do what I *provisionally assume* is good for me.

Knowing I can never be sure that I am not deceiving myself gives me a greater practical ability to be open to things I cannot imagine, things that may unfold in the next moment. I will likely miss some of the wonders of life if I have convinced myself I have arrived at a level of insight where self-deception is no longer a possibility.

Practically speaking, I make my choices based only on what I find compelling; I cannot be certain whether or not I will be *ultimately correct*. But this may be auspicious. Not being completely sure of anything, and particularly remaining open to the possibility of grossly deceiving myself, might allow me to peek into worlds well beyond my imagination.

6

Apophatic flaw

"If your argument is air tight,
it probably has a fundamental flaw."
Rawley Creed

By now some readers may have noticed a flaw in the apophatic scheme. If one is to maintain complete openness, that would seem to necessarily include being open to not being open. And then one would next have to also be open to being open to not being open, etcetera, ad infinitum. Each apophatic claim requires maintaining openness, and hence it logically requires making an additional subsequent claim which will undercut its own validity. One is drawn into what Michael Sells calls an "eternal regression."[1]

There appears to be no final cure for this philosophical quandary.[2] But, having no solution for it can turn out to be a good thing; it can be useful to practice an approach which quite plausibly contains an inescapable flaw. It might lessen the temptation for the apophatic practitioner to sell his *perfect practice* to everyone else. Having a major flaw in one's thinking is an excellent source of spiritual poverty.

In any case the problem can be practically and temporarily, if not logically, overcome. This is accomplished by adding the word *optimum* or *optimally*. Thus I would say *optimally open*. Here the aim is not complete openness, which seems to be philosophically untenable, but rather an *optimal sense* of openness. And so please add that word whenever my text implies or explicitly suggests there could be a perfect openness, or a *perfect* anything. In apophatic practice, *perfect* is a four-letter word.

Apparently one must admit that a logically coherent and final statement describing the apophatic perspective cannot be obtained.

"What is most complete would seem to have something lacking."
Laozi, chapter 25

Notes:

1. Michael Sells offers an excellent, if provisional, solution in his book *Mystical Languages of Unsaying*, Michael A. Sells, The University of Chicago Press, 1994. See page 207.

2. Ibid.

7

Mysticism: what can we say?

Related to the problem of treating the subject of mystical openness and the confounding eternal regression is the question of saying anything definite about mysticism—or for that matter, anything else about this complex world of phenomena we inhabit.

If the ancient writing of Zhuangzi is accurate (and post-modern literary scholars seem to agree), it looks like nothing can be said about the human experience which would fit into a schematic that could claim to have overall coherence. It seems that every claim one tries to make contradicts some other claim that is just as compelling. The wise man is no more able to state truth with definitive finality than the fool. It looks like the best one can do is observe what seems to be occurring in one's world and make a gut response to it.

Laozi said, "The one who speaks does not know, the one who knows does not speak." In other words, if I assume I know exactly what I am talking about, that inflexible assumption will result in my losing the know-how with which I can best respond to what is actually happening around me. My claims of dogmatic knowing will undercut my *knowing-how*. Dogmatic knowing makes for a static position and the apophatic know-how depends on flexibility. Giving up dogmatic claims is hard for the human being. We dearly want to know something for sure. And that is a desire which Zhuangzi says is best to be surrendered:

"Only when there is no yearning for analytic conclusiveness, will one realize the dao; only when there is no obedience to a secure position, will one find the tranquility of the dao; only when there is no set path or method, will one grasp the dao."

Zhuangzi, chapter 22

We apparently realize mystical ability by knowing how to engage and apply it, not by knowing what it is. Thinking that we do know what it is reduces our ability to grasp it.

8

Spiritual poverty

"I have shed the idea of my being a clever, sagacious and spiritually arrived sage. If you call me an ox, I will assume it to be so. If you call me a horse, I will take your words to be honest. If a person makes a characterization of something and I refuse to accept their view, I injure myself twice. I surrender my viewpoint categorically; I don't surrender only when I think there is a rational proof that I should."

Zhuangzi, chapter 13

In every dialogue Zhuangzi defers to the possible validity of others' beliefs, first of all because he does not have any fixed belief or disbelief of his own; another's belief is as good as anything he might conclude, if he ever tried to conclude something. But Zhuangzi also suspects he can't conclude anything with certainty. From his point of view, not only might he be an ox as the other person claims, but what he actually is and what his existence means may also turn out to be even worse than an ox. He wants to avoid ruling out anything so that he can enter each moment ready for the unimaginable quality and circumstance that are found there.

What Zhuangzi seems to mean by "twice injuring" himself is that when he disagrees with the other person, he loses both his spiritual poverty (i.e., he mistakenly is certain he knows something) and his opportunity to intimately engage another person. The ecstatic engagement of his world and every being in it depends on his ability to maintain spiritual poverty.

Zhuangzi discovered one of the strangest and most profoundly hidden secrets of mysticism. The ability to realize that the ability to be completely wrong is essential to mystical freedom and to the ability to be intensely present to one's world. One never wants to lose this powerful skill.

So far I have found it useful to not make any final conclusions about my experiences nor characterize them as true or untrue. I don't assume there is any permanent essence in anything; in my view there might be and there might not be. But if someone else regards something to be absolutely and eternally true, I find no reason to question their belief. Their idea of truth is as good as any guess I might make about any particular thing being true or untrue. That is because I have no clue as to the truth of anything beyond my current moment of experience. To the degree that I am able to realize I don't have a clue about any everlasting truth, to the degree that I can keep from fooling myself by a mistaken belief that I could have a clue, I will be able to remain spiritually poor. Spiritual poverty is what keeps my psychic field free of obstructions; this poverty of having no truth allows each previously unknowable moment to open up in the splendor of its own raw immediacy.

"Fortunate are the poor in spirit."[1]
Jesus of Nazareth

The mystic's interest is the sustenance gained from the intimate communication which is maintained through continual receptivity. In a conversation he finds no need, unless forced, to express doubts about the claims of another person. Argument is generally a gratuitous activity. If the other person expresses a differing view, there are a number of other more useful things that can be said in reply. Complicating an encounter with needless argumentation does not serve a useful purpose.

Even if what another person proposes appears to be absurd, the mystic does not want to rule it out. In comparison with the magnitude of what is actually occurring in this moment of existence, there is probably very little distance between another person's claims about reality and my own. By focusing my attention on our differences, I lose my grasp of something much grander than the cognitive capacity of either of us. Losing that grip on the jewel, I lose the most remarkable potential of a human's ability. I lose my connection with the other person, as well as with the unimaginable. That is a double injury which Zhuangzi avoids.

For the open-hearted mystic, each moment of being is a surprise. He is astounded simply by the very existence of the moment now at hand.

Notes:

1. Matthew 5:3. All of my citations from Jewish and Christian scriptures are taken from *The Holy Scriptures: A New Translation from the Original Languages* by J. N. Darby (London: G. Morrish, 1890). This text is in the public domain. I am not using any other translations of these Scriptures, for example citations from Hebrew Bibles (the Tanakh), because of copyright restrictions. In the notes I will hereafter refer to the Darby text as "The Holy Scriptures."

9

An alien abduction

If I cannot provisionally suspend my belief system—in particular my assumptions about my motives for holding on to those beliefs—I will not be open to perceiving significant things that may occur in my perceptual field. I will miss experiencing these things because I will have been busy consciously or unconsciously defending my beliefs. This defense causes a severe narrowing of my vision.

Defensiveness is particularly relevant in encounters with other believers, which is to say, every human being you and I will ever meet. We all have a myriad of beliefs and disbeliefs (disbeliefs being only another form of belief). We all are fundamentalists of one kind or another.

One day a woman, let's call her "Clare," told me that years ago on a late August afternoon she had been abducted by alien beings from outer space. I listened attentively while she described what she could recall about her abduction and transport off of this planet. Before she got very far, she asked me what I thought about such stories. Her tone of voice and facial expression were asking if I believed her story was "real."

I replied that in my world I did not know how to determine what was real and what was not; however, it seemed to me that the reality of something could only be authenticated by the person who experienced it. I

31

said it was obvious to me that what happened to her was a remarkably significant event, but I felt unqualified to speculate on the question of its universal validity. Nor, in fact, did I imagine that I could ever know with certainty the validity of any other kind of report, whether mundane or extraordinary, that had been given to me by another human.

What I said appeared to satisfy her; I seemed to have passed a test.

Clare's story was brief; she told of being grabbed by unseen assailants and then forced through the door of something she took to be a flying vehicle of some sort. She was unable to recall any of the details of her time in captivity, only remembering that it was a period of "sheer terror."

Whatever the ordeal was, when it ended she found herself sitting in a newly cut wheat field not far from her house. She could not recall how she had been deposited there. "But," she told me, "I understood that something nearly fatal but important for me had occurred during my time with them." When she was finished with her story she thanked me and said, "Your listening has helped me a lot."

Clare's abduction story has mythical authenticity for me, which is not to say that I believe it to be either "real" or "illusionary." To say it is mythical is to simply say that it reveals something true about the fluid state of affairs which exists at the ground of being; or at least at the ground of my being, and maybe yours too. It is quite useful for me to be able to obtain a report about this nearly inaccessible realm, located so very far from my own reach.

Wherever Clare was taken to, it is not a place that I can easily go myself; however, I can obtain a small glimpse of a rarely experienced psychic landscape through her report. We can translate her account and use it to locate some of our own deeply hidden landscapes. Perhaps Clare is the shamaness who plunges into heaven and hell for the rest of us. Returning, we find that she has graciously brought back a priceless map to share.

My point here is that if I am not extremely open, emotionally and conceptually, I will probably not obtain and reap the benefits of these uncanny reports. I apparently did something useful for Clare by listening, and it is obvious to me that she did me a lot of good.

I want to carefully and open-heartedly listen to your reports as well. In between the lines of your story is likely to be the next myth that I need to find, a secret which can further penetrate the terrible beauty of my own world.

10

Self and ego

"Why do I give up my preoccupation with my self?
Simply to get more benefit for myself."
Laozi, chapter 7

In a number of mystical traditions the "self" is treated as an illusion. These folks say that there is actually no self. It may be that there is no "self" as the term is commonly understood, and yet I think the word has practical usefulness. I see the self as a process, a changing phenomenon whose activity is generated by a unique semi-autonomous agent. This agent and its unique experience consist of a nexus of integrated self-reflection and responsiveness. This nexus has both innate and learned preferences, and behaves according to these preferences. It is a process which is motivated to help itself continue to thrive. It does not seem to independently exist, and yet appears to be as "real" as any other phenomenon.

The ego

In historical discussions of mysticism the "ego" is something that is often referred to as a thing to get rid of. But in terms of its original Freudian definition, the ego is essential to life. In Freud's terms the ego is the entity that organizes the perceptions of, and the responses to, the human being's world. If there is a fire in the house the ego's cognitive facility estimates the danger and the best way to put out the fire and/or escape. The ego is the maker and regulator of self-perspective. In this sense of the word, the ego is something we continually need to successfully navigate our world.

The ego that effectively identifies a doorway later becomes a dictator who insists I always use that same doorway.

The ego does not only construct a stable conceptual framework for its collection of experiences. From its experiences of pleasure and pain, it assigns corresponding values to various aspects of the structure. These self-imposed values later become one of the most difficult things to give up when one desires to achieve mystical ecstasy, the escape from the limits of the self.

As we progress in life experience the ego begins to take on additional tasks whose value we might begin to question. It begins to sense a need to assert our individual value as measured against the value of others. And it begins to assume a role of devising schemes that we believe can reliably bring us an increasing enjoyment of life. This is to say, the ego attempts to control the various circumstances that produce happiness.

The mystic seeks a way of happiness that is not dependent on circumstances. And so for the mystical method to succeed, the ego needs to let go of much of its predominant role in the pursuit of happiness. The mystic reigns in the ego's attempt to contrive happiness, knowing that it is the intuitional facility of the psyche, not the contingency-dependent ego, which is capable of realizing a nearly continual mystical ecstasy. Getting the ego to let go of its control of the happiness-task is the daunting work of mystical cultivation.

Constructing and maintaining a sense of self-worth

The individual learns to obtain his sense of self-worth from the values he constructs, with the help of his social network. He implicitly assigns absolute values to some of these acquired preferences. His ego develops a particular fondness for the truth of the beliefs which it has chosen to describe the self and its world. These "absolutely true" values become nearly impossible to modify, even when they no longer prove to be useful.

If I am quiet enough and open enough, I will inevitably see things in my self that I would rather not see. Some of the things I will see will devastate a number of ideas that I have about my self. Later I may be able to see the benefits obtained in deconstructing my self-image and putting it back together on different ground. But in the meantime reconstructing the ego is a tricky process with opportunities for a number of nasty surprises.

Da fang: The greater perspective

To achieve the creative power inherent in what Zhuangzi calls the *da fang* (great view, or the aperspectival view), I must overthrow the tightly held dominance of my ego's limited individual perspective, and realize the efficacy of a much larger view. The ego's organization of the perceptual field inevitably alters and reduces the richness of that field. Mystical experience involves deconstructing much, but not all, of the ego's careful work. This dismantling and reconfiguration of psychic processes, if successful, will put the ego into a much more *subordinate and useful* place. [1]

Over the years, the ego's narrow point of view has firmly established itself at the center of my awareness;

to anchor this center the ego's censors carefully filter all the incoming data from my perceptual field. The censors eliminate a wealth of potentially useful material as they weed-out anything that is unfavorable to my self-image. And so my point of reference toward the world becomes an impoverished self-deception, providing me with a tiny view of what is occurring in and around me.

"That is like trying to look at the breadth
of the sky through a reed."
Zhuangzi, chapter 17

This pinhole view has resulted from my ego's narrow editing and organization of the perceptual field; it is based on how I mistakenly think I can best exploit the contents of that field. In my attempt at exploitation I am often opposing potentially useful and powerful forces in the field, forces which I wrongly think I need to vanquish. In actuality I would benefit more from the field if I was able to collaborate with, rather than directly oppose, the major currents that are operating in the field.

"The more I give to others,
the more I obtain for myself."
Laozi, chapter 81

I will find that I will get the most for myself by stepping outside my self-perspective to notice and respond to the needs and motivations of others.

The battle to free myself from my limited self-perspective presents me with both a conceptual problem and an intense emotional struggle. I need to re-conceptualize the world of my experience and overcome my anxiety about dealing with this less controllable world.

"She who defeats herself is truly strong."
Laozi, chapter 33

Nature has instilled a universal instinct within beings that moves them to seek self-improvement. In humans it becomes a conscious endeavor, a person becomes intent on running faster, baking the best bread, etc. The mystic might be tempted to claim to have become free of this "self-centered" goal-oriented motivation. But she is no different from the rest, even though her unusual aim is paradoxical: in her case her ego drives her to improve her ability to feel perfectly okay whether she ever improves at anything or not! And if she is able to realize that her fundamental motivations are ultimately just as mundane and self-serving as those of others, if she admits that she is also subject to the pleasure principle, she will have optimized her freedom to create unconditional happiness.

When a would-be mystic tries to completely eliminate the ego, if she is diligent and sincere, she will end up recognizing that her effort was actually only another attempt by her ego to aggrandize itself. Try to totally eliminate the ego and it will simply find a better place to hide. In fact I will transcend the narrow limits of my ego to the extent that I realize how absurd the idea of trying to eliminate the ego is.

The ego-pleasing paradox

Perhaps the most ego-pleasing idea of all is the thought that one actually could become completely free of all the plans, goals, values, and purposes of the ego! The inescapability of this irony might cause a person to laugh. From that cleansing laughter at the foolishness of the ego's pretensions, one might at least get relatively free from ego limitations.

Finding some measure of happiness in daily life is a challenge for all of us. The mystic takes the attainment of this natural desire to the limit of plausibility. She wants to be content nearly continuously! Such a huge order will require a major subordination of the ego.

The love of self is natural

"When I first realized how much I loved myself
I was horrified. But after I found out that
the disease was epidemic, I easily forgave myself."
Rawley Creed

By our nature we don't experience the other person as being as valuable as our own self. I am innately disposed to experience the value of another person largely in terms of his being useful or not to my purposes. This perspective is an unavoidable trait of human nature; it shows up quite naturally as the human being learns to estimate and exploit the benefits which it discovers in the surrounding world.

The mystic is able to get free of this limited notion of benefit and loss. She can step far enough out of herself (ecstasy) and see that her acquired habit of maintaining an estimate of her superior value is a contrived and unneeded farce. She is able to escape this limited self-perspective by laughing at her beloved conceit, while at the same time being careful to forgive herself for its natural but absurd self-evaluation. She gets free enough of herself to enjoy the value of you as a subject, not only as an object.

As the mystic engages you, she is simultaneously watching a mirror within her mind. In this mirror she notices herself and grins at her self-conceit; she is smiling at the banality and tenaciousness of her pretensions. The wider she grins at herself in the mirror, the more intimately she can engage you, and the more opportunity there is for each to enjoy the encounter.

Notes:

1. Zhuangzi writes of *crippled power*, which he says is the most effective mode of power. Perhaps that *crippling* means the ego (which we do need to organize the perceptual field) has been subordinated (crippled) under another mode by which we process our perceptions of our world. This other mode is non-linear mystical/intuitive. We are then free to do what Zhuangzi calls his *crooked walk*, which veers this way and that, overcoming the inconsistencies that arise with the ego's purely linear constructions.

11

Ecstasy

"She can find the same joy in one condition as well as she finds in another. That is to be freed from all care."
Zhuangzi, chapter 16

Mystical ecstasy is the experience of an intimate relationship, an intensification of the ongoing encounter between the person and the world he inhabits. It transforms the normal interactions of everyday life. The mystic is able to notice how astonishing the normal quality of this world actually is. Ecstasy changes the worldly relationship of "it and me" into a connection which is like that of mother and child.

During the period of ecstasy, the world that the mystic experiences, which had been seen at times as either friend or foe, is now a world where nothing that happens detracts from a nearly unshakable sense of well-being. As Zhuangzi puts it, the mystical adept "has a deep sense of well-being when he is materially successful, and also when he completely fails."[1] He finds a purpose in all seasons.

The word *ecstasy* in mystical literature indicates a "getting outside," going beyond the limits of one's normal ability to obtain contentment, and beyond one's normal inability to prevent discontentment. Here are the comments of Monica Sjöö and Barbara Mor who found the roots of the word ecstasy in Greek:

"Ecstasy is the dance of the individual with the All. Ekstasis means standing outside 'one's self,' and so canceling out the conditioned mind."[2]

Associated with the sense of stepping outside the self is a dramatic experience of visceral pleasure, a palpable flow of comforting internal sensations.

Mystical ecstasy might indicate an experience of something beyond the natural, but it also might be a natural phenomenon. Whichever one of these it is, ecstasy apparently results from a heightened mode of consciousness in which fear and anxiety are nearly vanquished by a temporal shift in awareness. In this shift the mystic's attention is drawn into and becomes entirely riveted within the experience of immediacy.

This heightened awareness leads to the discovery of some amazing contents and uncanny relationships which are always there to be found within each ordinary moment. Awed at what is simply happening right here, right now, the mystic's sense of the future is nearly erased. Fear, which depends on a strong sense of the future, becomes nearly impossible. With anxiety overpowered by the awe of the immediate, the heart opens and the mystic spontaneously falls in love with everything.

> "He does not allow the effects of the surpluses
> and losses occurring around him to enter his
> inner home, and so what could happen that
> would make him ill at ease?"
> *Zhuangzi*, chapter 19

Mystical ecstasy is not synonymous with joy. This ecstasy is a profound peace and affective sweetness that persists during both joy and sadness. The mystical experience during sad events continues to generate an underlying sense that the world is still working well, that gains and losses are both requisite for the animation of life, and that sadness and grief are authentic aspects of that animation.

There are different types and different intensities of pleasure. Pleasure can vary from uncontrollable joy to the feeling of comforting equanimity one may experience during sadness.

Emotional and cognitive integrity requires that one allow oneself to feel sadness when things happen that appear to be not at all beneficial. But even during the most tragically disturbing events, the mystic finds that the underlying core of peace and stability in his heart has not left him.

Ecstasy, as I and others have experienced it, and as I use the term here, is not the same as rapture. Rapture is a paroxysm of joy. Rapture may be mystically efficacious or not. The mystical adept may regularly or rarely experience it. The apophaticist neither emphasizes nor denigrates the rapture experience. Rapture is just fine, but it is not his principle aim.

In his superb study of mysticism William James said, "Mystical states cannot be sustained for long. Except in rare instances, half an hour, or at most an hour or two, seems to be the limit beyond which they fade into the light of common day."[3] In his book James admits he is not a mystical adept, and yet the reader will find that James' actual understanding of the subject is excellent. From my point of view James' description of mystical states as non-enduring misses the mark. I think he is referring to what we are defining here as rapture, not mystical ecstasy. Mystical ecstasy endures for various lengths of time and to various degrees of intensity.

Mystical ecstasy occurs as often and as intensely as you exercise your ability to *step outside* your conditioned or small self and open to the greater perceptual field that is out there. I have met people who are *outside* most of the day. Stepping outside is an ability that can be greatly increased.

Mystical ecstasy has some rational elements in it, but it is for the most part a non-rational phenomenon. That is to say, one's sense of well-being is not explainable in rational terms. One might accurately say that the mystic is content for no reason. Or if there is a rational reason hidden somewhere in the depths of the psyche, it is not knowable. In contrast to the Christian Bible, here we have a case of a mystery, not an obvious truth, "that sets one free."

A handy rule of thumb: A virtual lack of resentment is an indication of enduring mystical ecstasy.

However, resentment is not the same as regret. Material loss produces an emotional sense of loss (i.e., regret), and we do need a sense of gain and loss to safely negotiate our world. Safe choices require that we accurately remember some of our past choices as being materially useful or not. I need to be able to remember, which is to say I need to regret, the morning that I was badly burnt when I picked up a frying pan without a potholder. But when regret becomes resentment, it causes distress and damage at a deeper level. During mystical ecstasy there is scarcely ever a trace of resentment about anything.

Ecstasy is not a selfless occupation; it is the relocation of self-interest into a vastly larger field, a field of splendor that extends beyond the imagination. Ecstasy is stepping outside the self to embrace the unimaginable.

The mystical adept looks as candidly as possible at his own motives and concludes that the best way to characterize his behavior is to say he is seeking the greatest pleasure, and not necessarily a "greatest good." Pleasure seeking is subjective and individual, while "good" purports to be objective and universal. The adept suspects that he cannot determine what this universal "good" might be. He also suspects that this notion of objective "good" will falsely separate beings into categories of noble and ignoble, beings whose preciousness he senses to be immutably equal.

In a nutshell

Mystical ecstasy describes a disposition of mind and body, achieved for a certain period of time, in which a person has nearly, if not completely, eliminated emotional distress no matter what the current circumstances. One has been delivered out of one's normal human perspective. The deliverance results in a pervasive sense of well-being, sometimes mildly serene and at other times joyfully rapturous.

Ecstasy: It could happen to you

"It was around 5:30 p.m. on a typical summer evening in the Washington, D.C. area. That means hot and humid with the usual forecast of thunderstorms. I was watching the news when the emergency broadcast system broke in with that annoying alarm that signals the possibility of a dangerous situation. A tornado had been spotted approximately 3 miles from my home and I was being advised to seek shelter immediately in a basement or interior room. I have no basement, so that was not an option. The only interior room is a small powder room. My husband decided the safest place for us was our garage. He felt the steel beam would remain intact in the event the tornado touched down. We hurriedly grabbed a transistor radio and headed for the garage to wait it out. While there, I had one of the strangest experiences of my life. My mind always operates in overdrive, with at least ten different thoughts bombarding it at any given time: what I have accomplished, what I am doing, what I am going to do, what I should be doing, etc. But this time my complete focus was on the tornado heading in our direction. After about twenty minutes, the danger had passed. When I returned to the house and my mind shifted back into its normal overdrive mode, I suddenly realized what I had just experienced. For the first time that I can recall, my mind was clear of all extraneous thoughts and I had existed totally "in the moment." This was the most exhilarating feeling of freedom I had ever known. I am not hoping for another tornado scare, but I would certainly welcome the experience of totally decluttering my mind again."

Virginia Coscia

Notes:

1. *Zhuangzi*, chapter 28.

2. Monica Sjöö and Barbara Mor, *The Great Cosmic Mother; Rediscovering The Religion Of The Earth*, Harper-Collins, San Francisco, 1987, page 52.

3. William James, *The Varieties of Religious Experience,* Collier Books, New York and London, 1961.

12

容 Rong: the all-embracing

"To be honest with you, I am only interested
in love. I don't want to be bothered with
faith or hope."
                                Carla Ansantina

The mystic's love, in my experience, includes both
the typical human being's *particular love* and an
underlying all-embracing love which is ubiquitous. In
the mystic's case, the preponderant sense of love that
occurs is the latter. By *particular love*, I mean love
which expresses an intense attachment to a particular
person or animal. This could be a friend, lover, cat, dog,
etc. All-embracing ubiquitous love is more generic, like
the case of "She loves eating." However, in the case of
the mystic's love, there is a wider scope; she experiences an unreasonable, non-rational enjoyment of
everything. Particular love is not absent when love
becomes ubiquitous, but rather is subsumed within the
all-embracing.

Love what you hate *or* Loving hate

The mystic smiles appreciatively at all things,
including her own anger and anxiety. In apophatic
mysticism, love does not mean you don't hate anything;
it rather means you embrace, at a deeper level, even
that which you hate. The daoist mystics call this *rong*,
the all-embracing. To embrace all is to embrace the
value of the world in its totality and to sense the
presence of immutable value in every other being. At

the root of your psychic substance, what the daoists call the *inner heart,* you treasure the world as it is and all of its beings no matter what they do. Sensing that other beings have an existence as precious as your own, it is easy to receive each of them with as much graciousness as personal safety will allow.

In mystical love you enjoy the chocolate, but everything else as well. This is the mystical ecstasy, the arising of an effortless and inexplicable fondness for all things. We can't do this kind of loving on command or by volition; it has to happen to us.

"Love your enemies."[1]
Jesus of Nazareth

We are inevitably going to have opponents; there will be situations where the material well-being of other people and other beings is inconsistent with our own. Loving these adversaries means appreciating their value and realizing that their desires might be just as legitimate as our own. It does not mean not harming them. Mystical love has different degrees of passion and different modes of expression, but no matter what degree and form it takes, its non-contingency is the constant. The enemy and the friend are treated with as much respect and concern as is practical and can be safely expressed.

In taking a life, animal or human, the apophaticist appreciates a level of value in the one who is harmed which is identical to the value of his own life. We can see this awkward proximity of mystical love and the pragmatic need to cause harm in a chapter of the *Laozi.* As in modern times, most people of his time believed that there were legitimate occasions for going to war. But in contrast to both modern and ancient convention, after winning a battle Laozi advises the soldiers not to

48

celebrate the victory, but rather to allow themselves a natural shedding of tears for the fallen enemy.

The mystic realizes a sense of immutable affection toward every being and toward everything that he experiences. This affection is not sensed as a moral imperative; it is rather the experience of a gift freely given. For the apophaticist, unconditional love is not a doctrine to follow; it is a phenomenon spontaneously generated when the heart has been emptied of everything that had limited it. As Zhuangzi says, it arises naturally when the mind is freed from all of its pre-judgments.

Love and self-value

貴在於我而不失於變

"Your preciousness lies in your essence;
it cannot be lost by anything that happens."
Zhuangzi, chapter 21

Almost from the day you are born the teaching begins: your worth will depend on how you behave and what you produce. It is a useful teaching; your community, both family and tribe, depend on your usefulness. But something is lost when you learn this social skill.

Innocence was your birthright. With great effort, you can regain this gift, and once again hear a voice calling from the ground of your being. It is telling you of your immutable value, and assuring you that nothing can alter that preciousness. When you realize your perfect value again, you will treat both yourself and the rest of us much better.

Mystical love includes this sense of being loved; it is the offspring of the euphoria that occurs during mystical ecstasy. Ecstasy generates a feeling of unshakable well-being and that feeling generates love externally towards others. There is a sense of unconditional fondness for everything in the world of the mystic's experience. The personal sense of well-being and the unconditional sense of love are intricately connected. If nothing shakes my basic sense of well-being, I can maintain a positive attitude toward all of my experiences, even those which are quite unpleasant.

We are unconditionally valued by something we cannot see but whose compelling presence we can clearly sense, loved simply because we exist, not because of what we do or fail to do. It might be a cosmic force, or it might simply be an instinctive self-love instilled in us by nature.

"The adept embraces each and every being."
Zhuangzi, chapter 17

Mystical love is promiscuous. There is no being to be found anywhere who does not evoke the mystic's appreciation and affection; there is none whom he disdains.

"Love is not puffed up."
1 Corinthians 13:4[2]

Love has no station, it claims no status. The apophaticist is interested in love simply because it has been the most enjoyable thing he has found so far. He does not find love to be noble; in fact his sense is that the idea of nobility is a lie *against* love. A love that claims it is "good" has lost its heart.

A love increased by its very irrationality

When I speak of *unreasonable love* I am also saying that this love seems not to depend on one's having the certainty of any known metaphysical reason or meaning. Mystical love even appears to arise whether or not the mystic is certain that life makes any sense or has any fundamental purpose. The pragmatic apophaticist might imagine that there may be a good chance that life is completely meaningless, and yet this causes no dampening of her love for life.

Love happens and apparently can happen under any circumstance. The fact that love is enjoyable is the limit of the mystic's curiosity about it.

We have no proof that anything is actually the way we might think it to be. For example there is apparently no proof of the validity of theism or atheism, no proof of there being an ultimate meaning for the universe, and no proof of ultimate meaninglessness. And yet in the presence of this conceptual deficit we can experience a love that seems to be unconditional. I have yet to find anything that would conclusively justify this experience of unconditional love.

And therein lies a paradox. Practically speaking, it seems that having no justifying proof for the manifestation of this sense of astonishing love is exactly what generates its intensity. It apparently needs no reason for being. It seems that the less there is any reason for it, the more overwhelmingly potent it becomes. The imprudence of mystical love is shocking. It is indiscriminatingly gracious, hopelessly promiscuous. There is nothing it hates.

The quality of the mere momentary

Our experience of love becomes even more splendidly enjoyable when it loses any need for durability. It becomes a sublime experience when we realize that this love might have no lasting value. The fragile temporal-ity of the experience, the apparent inability of it to purchase anything beyond its moment, appears to be what makes the taste of it so wonderfully intense.

Mystical love is intimacy with one's world

As soon as there is an idea to defend, there is a restriction of consciousness. Consequently the potential for intimacy with one's world diminishes. The mystic does not want her beliefs distancing her from you. The mystic's only interest is ecstasy, and you are her best source.

無有入無間

Perhaps the most significant formula for the apophaticist is the one from chapter 43 of the *Laozi* which appears in the above Chinese. It can be interpreted as "The one who has no stuff is able to penetrate the one who has no openings." Another interpretation is "One who has no agenda can get through to one whose mind is closed." The formula demonstrates the high value the apophatic mystic places on openness and on the elimination of virtually anything that inhibits openness. The less I put between myself and my world, the more I can penetrate its profound mysteries and the more I will enjoy myself and all who dwell in my world.

Mystical love remains fully available whether one spends one's life stealing cars and shooting-up heroin or feeding starving people. And so one might ask: Why put any effort into deepening relationships with other beings? The answer is simple. For the mystic, there is no greater pleasure than an intimate encounter with another being. The root cause of the mystic's behavior is pleasure; it is not a desire to please an internal or external demand for "good" behavior. The mystic feels no such demand from *whatever it is* that is constantly showering him with a sense of love. Its love is non-contingent.

Notes:

1. The Holy Scriptures: Matthew 5:3.

2. Ibid., 1 Corinthians 13:4.

13

A double-view of the world

Zhuangzi describes the mystic as having *a double-view* and a *double-walk:*

> "His unity makes him a disciple of the heavenly.
> His disunity (ability to discriminate differences)
> makes him a disciple of the human. He allows
> neither the heavenly nor the human to
> extinguish the legitimacy of the other.
> Such a fellow is called the consummate person."
> *Zhuangzi*, chapter 6

Zhuangzi's *unity* is the ability to process perceptual data intuitively and with an impartial aperspectival view. His *disunity* gives him the ability to process data with the application of cognitive discrimination. He won't call a thief good or evil (unity), but may still see the need to put the fellow in jail (discrimination).

Zhuangzi says that a mystical adept does a *double-walk*. The mystic processes her world simultaneously from *both* a unified aperspectival, or nonjudgmental point of view *and* a point of view that legitimizes the separation of values and desires of different individuals. She sees an indivisible whole while also recognizing different situations. She sees both a world where one thing is as worthy as another, but at the same time where material survival necessitates discrimination and critical choices. Psychologically, she sees both intuitively and analytically. Ethically, she sees amorally and morally at the same time. This often requires affirming the validity of two apparently conflicting viewpoints.

14

What is it worth to you?

> "When you are in a shooting contest to win tiles you concentrate and your skill is consummate; but when you are shooting for decorative belt buckles your nerves get edgy. Shooting for gold completely unglues you. Your skill did not change, but external concerns weighed heavily on your mind. Whenever you put too much attention on the outside you become awkward inside."
>
> *Zhuangzi,* chapter 19

One of the greatest challenges in the practice of mysticism is developing a more flexible, honest, and effective approach to values.

My ability to achieve and maintain mystical ecstasy hinges on how I deal with questions of values, particularly ethical values. An inept application of values will lead me to imprudently respond to what is happening in the world around me. Mystical ecstasy requires an intimate, congruent, and sensitive responsiveness to that world and all the beings within it.

Let's look at general values first.

If I overly value a particular outcome, I markedly reduce my openness and flexibility. I limit that mystical skill which can find usefulness even in unwanted experiences. Distracted by wanting something else, or wanting to be somewhere else, I forgo the rewards of ecstatic presence. But if I am able to realize value in even those things which I think are negative, I will be discovering what Zhuangzi calls finding the "use of the useless." Indeed, I will often find the *useless* turning out to be the most useful thing of all.

When the mystic has learned how to make use of everything, she will be able to experience continual ecstasy; this is what Zhuangzi calls "making a springtime of everything..."

> "The adept summons harmony and well-being from all circumstances; she notices they are all connected and does not dismiss the value of what she hates. Day and night she realizes this, thus she can make a continual springtime with everything that happens. Her heart greets the birth of every moment. This is called power undivided."
>
> *Zhuangzi*, chapter 5

The problem with evaluating the worth of objects and events is that we become inflexibly attached to specific values. We often assume that whatever was useful in our past experience will surely continue to be useful now. We become attached to our ideas of what is beneficial and what is not. What we are attached to might be either material or non-material. We might be attached to being able to drive a car, or we may be attached to a religious belief—or attached to the idea that all religious beliefs are implausible.

It is useful to be continually asking ourselves, as my friend Scott Railsback reflects: "Is this value I hold serving me now?"

Trying to be good

The human being finds it advantageous to establish moral guidelines and often assumes these to be absolute laws. Such rules are necessary to maintain social stability. There is a second motive for establishing what is considered morally right and morally wrong. This is the desire of the human animal to establish its sense of self-worth. The human is deeply preoccupied with this project. And this human has found through experience that the handiest way to establish self-value is to develop a scale of moral worth with which it can favorably compare itself to other humans. If I can feel that I am morally better than you, I feel much better about myself...or so I might believe.

Holding inflexibly to ethical values is one of the most common factors preventing mystical ecstasy.

The apophatic mystic takes an approach to ethics and morality which is similar to that with which she considers all other issues. She is pragmatic; she asks herself: "To enjoy life do I need to prove to myself that I am better than others? If I attempt to demonstrate to myself that I am morally superior to others, will the actual result be self-deception? How does what I am proposing affect my ability to mystically engage the world of my experience?"

Which constituents in my mind, including moral and other kinds of outlooks, hamper mystical ecstasy? Which views that I harbor reduce the level of intimacy I can attain with my world?

Please note that I am *unpacking* the general principles that underlie the data with which the mystic is working. Most of the time, she is consciously unaware of behaving in accordance with these principles. She usually does not "think through" her perceptions and responses; she acts intuitively, not analytically. What I am presenting underlies the subconscious decision-making processes.

The evolution of the mystic's attitude toward ethics begins as she looks at her place in the world that surrounds her and notices that it is a place which contains a myriad of beings with differing individual interests. The man wants to eat the fish, and the fish wants to eat the man. And just among the humans alone, there are a multitude of mutually exclusive interests. These mutually exclusive interests all appear legitimate; their claim to legitimacy depends solely on which side's point of view one takes in a particular conflict. This view of the ethical landscape is well captured in the words of Liezi:

> "There are no absolute principles, no actions that are wrong from every perspective. You can't fix a right and wrong that suit all cases."
> *Liezi*, chapter 9

In other words, at first glance, all ethical values seem to be relative. They vary according to your point of view. Few events in this world appear to have a clear, consistent positive or negative value from an *aperspectival* view. An aperspectival view would have to include the view and interests of each and every being.

> "Steal a buckle and they will execute you. Steal a nation and they make you a prince."
> *Zhuangzi*, chapter 10

Ethical decisions seem to rely largely on context; almost any choice is legitimate given the right time and place. The determination of what is ethical depends on whose interests are served.

But then, with more reflection the mystic realizes that her sense of ethical relativity might only describe her world. It does not necessarily reflect the other person's experience. Furthermore, she notices that there is an inherent contradiction in the idea that "all values are relative."[1]

"There is evil, and there is not."
Maria Martinez

The mother who has lost a child, especially a child whose death is due to the violent act of another person, may feel that what has happened constitutes an absolute evil. And that characterization is apt for the trauma she has experienced. The world she inhabits is a world which she, like the rest of us, has constructed from direct and from culturally transmitted experience. It is her reality. Who is the outsider who would tell her she is wrong? And to what end? It seems that there is neither a conclusive philosophical warrant nor a practical reason to contradict this mother's assessment.

The mystic reflects on what she sees happening around her and has the sense that she cannot conclusively assert that there are absolute values, but she equally cannot conclude there are none. Furthermore, she notices that if she did conclude that only one of these two opposing ideas could be true, this would distance her from those who disagree with her. Most importantly, she would also distance herself from the apparently inconsistent, but nevertheless compelling world of her own experience. She would distance herself from the deep peace within her own self.

Strangely enough, the mystic finds that she can proceed quite well through her world without reaching any final conclusions on the matter of absolute versus relative ethics. She entertains the plausibility of both of these two apparently contradictory ethical paradigms and finds peace through accepting the paradox.

When a moral question arises, she can pragmatically integrate and apply all the available data. Her pool of data includes a multitude of dynamic variables. She looks at what is going on, assesses the plausibility of differing moral viewpoints, intuitively integrates her perceptions, then responds prudently. She does not see her response in terms of right or wrong. The best that can be said is that she senses her response to be facilitating local harmony. By facilitating local harmony I mean that the mystic's behavior is usually seen to be of benefit to her immediate family and local community. (It might not, however, be of benefit to outsiders.)

Avoiding the temptation to finalize and embrace a comprehensive ethical model allows the mystic to be honest with herself. As Laozi says, "One must be crooked in order to be straight." To have optimal internal integrity, one best not insist on a world that makes perfectly logical ethical sense.

An effective response to the ethical sensitivity of another person is readily achieved when one accepts the notion that coherent and aperspectival ethical norms are probably not obtainable. Neither an exclusively fundamentalist view nor an exclusive moral relativism provides an outlook that permits mystical resonance with another person.

"You can't be good, but you can be prudent
about inflicting your goodness and badness."
Carla Ansantina

Given the irreconcilable ethical contradictions that one faces in life, trying to be good with consistency is an implausible and thus a humbling endeavor. Therein lays part of its mystical value. To her chagrin, the mystic discovers she can do *no better than anyone else* when it comes to firmly establishing the plausibility of her own moral goodness. She can act prudently within her family and local society, but it seems she cannot do *good* from an aperspectival point of view. Whatever *good* is done for one being here will inevitably cause an expense for another somewhere else.

Amorality: The mother of universal love?

Language gets tricky here. By taking an amoral position, I mean that I am not insisting that there are moral absolutes. But it also means that I am not insisting that there are none. The amoral position leaves the question open. The mystic finds that this openness is spiritually efficacious.

Nonattachment to moral finality serves the mystic well when she encounters another. By refraining from definitive judgment about the worth of other people or the value of their behavior, the mystic practitioner becomes more fully available for a spontaneous and mutually beneficial encounter. The mystic's lack of adverse moral judgments is sensed on some level by the other person; it registers consciously or unconsciously in their psyche. This then increases their propensity to communicate with sincerity and candor. With intimate communication the ground has been laid for the level of mutual affection that commonly ensues.

Empirically it turns out that, as Zhuangzi says, a natural affection spontaneously arises whenever a human being meets another creature to whom she has applied no preconceived moral assessments. Because of her amoral perspective, the mystic responds to every being she meets, for example poisonous snakes, with a combination of pragmatic carefulness and benign impartiality. She finds herself similar to some children, spontaneously fond of all beings.

Intimacy and reliability

Closely related to the issues of values and ethics is the matter of interpersonal reliability. Intimacy requires behavioral reliability, that is to say predictability. The human being distances himself from those people (and other beings) whose behavior is erratic. This alone is enough to cause the mystical adept to acknowledge the legitimacy of, and to incorporate, certain social norms.

Zhuangzi believed that even if one might find no warrant for the possibility of establishing consistently and coherently fair laws, one would still find that laws are a legitimate need of human society. He said, "Laws are for order, not for obtaining ultimate fairness." (*Zhuangzi*, chapter 14)

Leaving the ethical dilemma unsettled

The problem inherent in morality is described by H. J. Blackham as "the inexpurgatory ambiguity of good and evil."[2] This dilemma has not been solved by moral philosophers. The apophatic mystic also leaves the problem unsettled. She does not hold to the idea that there are absolute values and fixed ethical truths, and she does not hold that there are not. It is this very unsettledness of the moral equation which gives the mystic the flexibility to make pragmatic decisions while continuing to embrace the precious value she senses within every being.

The apophaticist, while finding that conventional ethical models do not work for her, also inconveniently finds no workable replacement. She is not wedded to conventional morality, but she does consider moral judgments to be data that plays a legitimate role in the lives of human beings. Moral data, like all data, is given due consideration. As with any other data it is intuitively weighed against all the other data, regarded and disregarded according to the needs of the situation, then integrated into her choices and responses to events.

Prudence

The apophaticist is prudent with regard to those things which are germane to her mystical endeavor. It is not that she has sensed an absolute moral imperative to be prudent. She has simply found that prudence, most particularly in personal relationships, leads to a more intimate communication and understanding, and thus deepens the potential for mystical ecstasy.

It is prudent for the mystic to understand that if other people take something as a moral imperative, she is best to accept that imperative as something which is an authentic experience for that person. For all she knows, it is just as likely to be as authentic for them as any of her own experiences are for her, even though it is something very different from what she has experienced.

Applied ethics

In June of 2008, I decided that the discussion of ethics in this book would benefit if I added some practical examples. To that end I sent two thousand dollars to International Children's Heart Foundation (babyheart.org) to cover the incidental costs of heart surgery for an infant child from northern Africa. The members of ICHF's surgical teams donate their precious labor.

I also sent another two thousand dollars, half of which was provided by my sister Joyce Dalman, to Children's Shelter of Cebu (cscshelter.org) to cover the supplementary expenses of reconstructive plastic surgery for a nine-year-old Filipina.

My interest here is to explore some ethical issues related to these donations. At the time of my donations, I could have comfortably paid for five or ten more lifesaving heart surgeries. What are the ethical implications of not doing that? Is letting these other unknown children die when I could have easily saved their lives an ethical failure? What is the difference between killing a human being and letting a person die whose life I could save? Is there any difference between directly observing someone who will die if nothing is done for him and doing nothing to prevent that death, and letting some faraway stranger die, a child who I could have easily saved by covering the cost of surgery on her congenitally defective heart?

I have a friend whose family expenses leave him with little or nothing to spare. He has a daughter who is attending a rather expensive university. He could have her transfer to a community college and reallocate those funds to save a number of infants with congenital heart defects. Is it a moral transgression if he does not do so?

What are the moral ramifications of donating the money as I did in this case with the ulterior motive of using the examples in an essay about morality? Is it less ethical than money given with no ulterior motive? If so, should I not have done as I did?

Should I have felt resentment in 1970 when a driver recklessly caused a truck to hit my motorcycle, spilling me onto the freeway in San Clemente, California? And what might a mother on the other side of the world think if she learned that I allowed her child to die for want of the funds needed for heart surgery?

It was questions like these that caused Zhuangzi to doubt whether he could conclude any final judgments which could be deemed to be ethically coherent. He saw that those of us who conformed to the ethical sensitivities of our families and local community are probably nevertheless unable to honestly find a universal moral position from which we can justifiably condemn another person's behavior who does not conform to the local moral sensitivity.

A thief is jailed for his crime, but no one even thinks of jailing me for letting a child die on the other side of the world. One might say that difference in judgment for these two cases is based on common sense. But Zhuangzi saw that common sense is based on an arbitrary perspective that has the world's moral landscape carefully arranged in a manner that will allow me to feel good about my behavior and my character. It is not that Zhuangzi thought that the thief should not be put in jail; his point is that we cannot locate a universal morality where the thief can be shown to have done something materially worse than what the rest of us are regularly doing and failing to do. What the thief does upsets local harmony; this is a practical problem that is to be dealt with pragmatically. Zhuangzi sees a need for jailing a thief to preserve community's harmony, but at the same time recognizes the necessary and unavoidable hypocrisy which is always involved in such actions.

> "Judge not, and ye shall not be judged."[3]
> Jesus of Nazareth

Zhuangzi found that the adept was no better at finding coherent universal moral standards than anyone else. He saw that a sage would have the same problems in making consistent moral judgments as the common man. But seeing the (necessary) hypocrisy of the moral judgments made by human communities did allow Zhuangzi to step out of the typical human being's attitude of self-righteous derision toward the "law-breaker."

> "Right and wrong are hopelessly incoherent."
> *Zhuangzi*, chapter 2

Amoral virtue

Zhuangzi's conclusion after wrestling with the dilemma and not being able to obtain a coherent morality was rather unique; he discovered that it was exactly this *inability* to find a universally coherent pattern of ethical behavior which allowed the mystical adept to maintain her deep sense of equanimity and magnanimity towards all other beings. She has no disdain of any other human being because she realizes that from an aperspectival view she will generally behave with no better moral coherency than they do. If she were a jailer and you were a murderer, she would put you in jail without prejudice or disdain. She would have no problem jailing you, but would love you no less. That ability is the strange virtue of the double-view, intuitively integrating a sense of amorality and a sense of morality.

Notes:

1. To assert that "all values are relative" creates a logical problem, because the assertion itself can then only be relatively true.

2. H. J. Blackham: *Six Existentialist Thinkers*, The Macmillan Company, 1952. This old, short book is an enjoyable read.

3. The Holy Scriptures, op. cit.

15

Antinomianism

"I don't have any proof that anything is wrong.
But that doesn't say that everything is right. "
Rawley Creed

If you tell someone that the apophaticist espouses no fundamental *a priori* (absolute and eternal) ethical system, they often will mistakenly think that she must be an antinomianist.

Antinomianism is the idea that a person can legitimately find happiness by capriciously following his emerging desires, regardless of what others might think or how his choices or actions impact others.

Antinomianism is not the way of apophatic mystics. Although Zhuangzi did not subscribe to any fundamental ethical absolutes, he did recognize the legitimate practical value of socially constructed ethical norms. The apophaticist is sensitive to another person's relative sense of right and wrong, and that ethical information becomes part of the data which is integrated into his mystical praxis. He understands that the intimacy which he thrives on requires a careful consideration of other people's values. Given these aims, apophaticists cannot behave like antinomianists.

16

Gravity: ultimate value anxiety

> "...the third characteristic of religion is
> its claim for priority and seriousness,
> for which Paul Tillich uses the term
> 'ultimate concern.'"
>
> Walter Burkert [1]

One of the most difficult aspects of apophatic mysticism is freeing yourself from needing the certainty that you are doing something of significance, gravity, enduring value, and ultimate purpose. Religion and some forms of associated mysticism assure devotees that their individual existences will have a transcendent value if they act appropriately. Thus the advocates of these traditions assume they are dealing with issues of deep gravity, a gravity of which there can be no doubt.

It seems that even Marguerite Porete, the mystical queen of *nothing but love*, insisted she was dealing with something "real" and of unquestionable absolute importance.

In contrast, the pragmatic apophatic view encourages questioning the gravity of any enterprise. If I am completely sure that I am not participating in a folly, in an exquisite self-deception, then I am still holding on to something unnecessarily; I am still trapped by an unneeded need for certainty. I am still attached to my ego's value granting framework. My ego has a learned, perhaps natural and existentially driven, demand for significance and enduring value. Luckily this habit can be unlearned. The self can be taught that it can be perfectly content without knowing whether or not it has any enduring significance or ultimate worth. And, in fact, it will be ecstatic when it is free to act without this need.

To obtain optimal mystical know-how, I best laugh at my desire for significance and my need to insist that my mystical practice must be a vital reality. In that laughter I will be ecstatically freed from the limits of my ordinary self. I will then have traded away the assurance of a transcendent religious value for a *practical* value: the splendid joy of being fully available to what is here right now.

Notes:

1. *Creation of the Sacred, Tracks of Biology in Early Religions*, Walter Burkert, Harvard University Press, 1996.

17

Pragmatic and metaphysical

"As soon as you declare what something really is, you lose 95% of its useable value. Your mind has limited your use of the unspeakable part of the thing. How wise the ancients who forbid themselves to name God!"

Rawley Creed

When we deem something to have a metaphysical value, we are implying that it is a phenomenon with qualities which are universal, immutable, and eternal. Importantly, the apophaticist does not know whether his mysticism has this kind of metaphysical value or not. Answering the question either way would pose significant practical problems.

The apophaticist also avoids declaring apophaticism to have a metaphysical value. Like other mystics, the apophatic has had one, or a number of astonishing experiences. These extraordinary experiences might be explained by the existence of a metaphysical phenomenon. Or they might be explained by a phenomenon that is temporal and mutable. For all he knows, his mystical experience may be caused by a chronic self-deception. He is interested in its practical reliability, not its fundamental verifiability.

Because of the existential situation of the human being—a being who is conscious of its being but does not know where it ultimately came from or where it might be going—there seems to be a temptation to want to fix some kind of certainty to life, to find some primary aspect of this mystery that can be pinned down as *absolutely true*. We humans want to know things that are "really true."

There may be something about life that can be certified to be true, but the apophatic suspects the only thing he can prove about life is that he exists and is aware of his own existence. He can prove this merely by the definition of experience: experience is something that actually happens. (What he is in essence, however, might remain quite unknown.)

In other words, the mystic stands on shaky ground. He does not know if any other object or phenomenon has an ultimate (metaphysical) value. And yet he has strangely become surprisingly at ease with his ignorance, quite comfortable with this not knowing anything for sure. Of particular interest, he appreciates that his mystical approach, the center of interest in his life, might stop working at any time; he knows of nothing that could prove this impossible. Apophaticism might stop delivering him to ecstasy at any moment. It may be like a star that had shown for a billion years and then winked out one day.

The pragmatic apophatic mystic is motivated to practice mysticism solely because of what it brings to him right now in this moment. So far in his life, his staying in the moment has brought more than he needs for happiness; it has been of great practical value. It has been enough to cause him to lose any interest in the value of anything beyond this raw moment of wonder.

18

自樂: Self-generated well-being

"If you realize how to surrender to its dynamic principles you will be able to effectively respond to all eventualities and match every change as easily as if you were rolling a ball in your hand; you will have everything needed to generate your own happiness."

> From the postface chapter of the
> *Huainanzi*

At the heart of mystical ecstasy is a process which the ancient daoists called the self-generation of well-being. They termed it 自樂 (pronounced "zi luh"). This mystical dynamic is scarcely articulated in Western mysticism. It is somewhat similar to the uncanny formula of Meister Eckhart, which I rather perversely call "forcing grace." Eckhart tells us that if we line ourselves up with its principles, the divine has no choice but to generate blessings.[1]

Self-generated well-being indicates there is a continuing sense of contentment no matter what happens. The sense of well-being no longer depends on eventualities. Here, happiness has been entirely uncoupled from fate. *Self-generated* also indicates spontaneously arising, which is to say there has been no deliberate action taken to produce the ecstasy. It is self-generated by a falling into, or surrendering to, a particular mind-body disposition. This passive mystical disposition allows the adept to reap advantage from even the most materially negative events. Hence,

Zhuangzi says, "Where could I be sent that would not be just fine."[2]

Notes:

1. "...you should know that God must act and pour in as soon as he finds that you are ready. Do not imagine that God is like a carpenter who works or not, just as he pleases, suiting his own convenience. It is not so with God, for when he finds you ready he must act, and pour into you, just as when the air is clear and pure, the sun must pour into it and may not hold back. Surely, it would be a very great defect in God if he did not do a great work, and anoint you with great good, once he found you empty and innocent." *Meister Eckhart: A Modern Translation*, Raymond B. Blakney, (New York and London: Harper and Brothers Publishers), 1941, page 121.

2. *Zhuangzi*, chapter 6.

19

Cultivation

"There is nowhere to go but there are reliable ways to get there."
Rawley Creed

How can we achieve the mystical disposition that allows us to spontaneously generate our own contentment? This is the question of mystical cultivation. What know-how allows mystical ecstasy to occur?

Mystical cultivation aims at getting to and continually staying as close to the mystical threshold as possible, thus making the practitioner more frequently available to the effortless process which takes one across the threshold. When one is spontaneously pulled over that threshold, one is freed from the normal limits of self. Although I can't *do* anything to cause this breakthrough, I can cultivate my ability to be where I will receive it.

Through various methods of cultivation, the mystic can intentionally acquire the skill to collect attention and immerse it in the immediacy and fullness of the perceptual field. It is this concentrated awareness of the world inside and outside the skin that takes one to the mystical threshold. From there one is spontaneously transported into mystical presence.

The catch with cultivation is that if I am not sufficiently satisfied with my current state of perceived imperfection I will not be able to advance mystically.

This is because of the mystical paradox: I need to appreciate that I am already fundamentally just fine in order to improve my ability to enjoy myself.

I won't say too much about specific details of meditation; there is a wide variety of ways that work well. Take a class or look around a bookstore to begin your search. If you are sincere and open-minded, you will set an astonishing process into motion, a guidance system which will auto-direct you toward the ways and means you are seeking. This phenomenon, the self-directed process of realization, was called the "self-perfecting" by Zhuangzi. By following your intuition you will find every teaching you need at exactly the time you need it (and sometimes wishing you hadn't found it). If you don't find a suitable book on meditation, I suggest starting with Pema Chödrön's *The Wisdom Of No Escape*. It is excellent.

Hyperarousal: The dangers and benefits of putting nails through your palms

Some of us have found that mystical immediacy can be effectively cultivated through undergoing dramatically painful, erotic, and/or frightening experiences. Other less dramatic methods of hyperarousal are chanting, pleading prayer, prayer of gratitude, rigorous physical exercise, and shouting at the heavens. Exquisite pain as well as these other methods arrest the mind and quite promptly empty/open awareness, thus delivering a full attention to the moment. With full attention brought to the moment, one realizes the wonder that is continually unfolding in each moment. Mystical ecstasy is the engagement of that wonder.

After one has used states of hyperarousal a number of times to access the moment of ecstasy, one begins to register the "feeling" associated with the location where ecstasy is catalyzed. The location is now a retrievable psychic disposition; one knows how to find and re-access it, and can return to ecstasy without needing hyperarousal in the future. One can summon the mystical threshold with nothing more dramatic than the blink of an eye.

The problem with hyperarousal

The problem with cultivation through hyperarousal is that the ego loves to fill the *void* with exotically dramatic experiences. To the extent that you adorn your practice with exciting and even heroic forms and cultivation, you lessen the ability to dissolve the self into the more frequent ordinary moments of everyday life. To stay in the moment more continually, it is best to reduce the desire of the ego for excitement and self-aggrandizement, as much as possible. There is a practical advantage in cultivating mystical immediacy with something less dramatic and something which is more conveniently available: the contents and feel of each ordinary moment.

The ordinary moment is quite often found to be drearily prosaic. It can be pervaded with painful boredom for great lengths of time. But this very boredom and dissatisfaction can be usefully harnessed, cultivated, and transformed into an ability to nearly continually enjoy the immediacy of the moment. As the *Huainanzi* explains, when you have found out how to find satisfaction through dissatisfaction, you will be nearly continually satisfied.

One suggestion to experiment with this is when you feel bored, allow the bitter taste of that feeling to permeate your entire awareness; encourage it to proceed and sometimes even encourage it to escalate into anguish. Stop thinking of ways to escape boredom, and instead transfix your full attention on the intensity you will be able to develop within this feeling of dysphoria. With practice, the ugly feeling will not only dissolve, but it will also have become a most reliable generator of a deeper mystical disposition. You will find deliverance through the very prison in which your mind had entrapped you.

If you think you would benefit from some pain, direct your attention to the current moment. If pain is what you need, it will show up right here. No need for fasting or sitting on nails. Forcing yourself to sit with yourself in the immediacy of the moment is more useful and can be as painful or joyful as it needs to be.

The results of cultivation might not show up quickly, but over time you will achieve an ability to reach ecstasy nearly at will. The danger of using nails (dramatically exciting methods) is that the reliability of your access to ecstasy will be less reliable.

"The only thing you need to cultivate is immediacy."
Rawley Creed

Let me rant a bit more on this point. Dramatically moving practices, although they can effectively deliver one to the moment of ecstasy, pose two problems. First, they tend to be addictive; one may need ever more intense experiences to get the same level of ecstasy. Second, they tend to be attempts to fill the void. The ego does not trust emptiness and looks for what it thinks are more reliable ways to benefit the self.

The more exotic a form of cultivation, the more it impresses the ego as doing something significant. The ego is a natural reality builder, and so it is worried when nothing seems to be getting accomplished. And of course when nothing is getting done is exactly when the psyche is at the mystical threshold. If the ego keeps trying to fill the void, the ecstatic threshold will never be reached.

On the other hand

Not only can states of hyperarousal sometimes be effective in cultivation, but also certain practices such as singing, chanting, and dancing are transporters to ecstasy and are expressions and celebrations of ecstatic intimacy. Such practices are both the expression and results of shared affection.

For meditation—Stop making sense

To obtain the ineffable secret of non-contingency, you need to plunge into an occult zone of the psyche. What prevents us from going down there? Noise. The need is for inner stillness; the mind must stop making words. Anything that makes sense to the mind, especially the idea of values, is an obstacle. When we have fully stopped making sense, only feelings remain; at this point the plunge into the darkness accelerates. In the depths the treasure is found. When you grasp the jewel, you can take it back with you to your normal level of consciousness, and then there will no longer be much there that can take away your sense of well-being.

20

Reversing urgency

"Return to the one."
Zhuangzi, chapter 16

Rumi said we need to kill our urgency. The daoist found that one good way to kill it is to turn urgency back on itself. When a daoist returns to visceral awareness, if he finds urgency, he enters fully into the feel of it, and by doing so, regains awareness of the one undifferentiated void.

The sense of urgency is a feeling which occurs hundreds of times a day in various intensities. The grocery line seems too long; the Internet connection seems too slow. Alas, there are countless opportunities to practice reversing the flow of urgency.

Urgency and impatience have an emotional power that can be harnessed and used to cultivate mystical transformation. It can be easily, albeit painfully, noticed and focused on.

To take advantage of this state, first be on the lookout for urgency and impatience. Next, enter the feeling each time it occurs; urgency is an inner feeling of trying to get away from or get to somewhere else. The feeling is unpleasant, sometimes quite so, and becomes even more unpleasant when directly processed as in the following: Instead of trying to get away from the anxiety or vexation, focus on remaining in the unpleasant sense of urgency, go deeper into it by bringing your awareness further into it. Trying to become more aware of the feeling will at first be painful—it may even increase the feeling's intensity—but your focus will eventually reduce it. The transformation of the psyche is occurring both as the urgent feeling peaks and later even as the sense of urgency declines. Sometimes the reversal of emotional flow will almost instantly kill a sense of urgency.

When one reverses the flow, one is changing the inner neurological landscape, and the long-term outcome will be a more unshakable ability to rest in the subtleties of ecstasy. Five or six short episodes of reversing urgency are worth several hours of meditation. Note: Although it can be helpful for focus, you don't have to slow down external activity as you reverse urgency. You can be hurrying to finish a task and at the same time internally pushing more deeply into the feeling of urgency.

Consummation

The possibility of reaching a final enlightenment through mystical cultivation is reported in both historical and modern literature. Much of the reading intimates that one can finally reach a permanent and perfect mystical end state. This seems to me to be hyperbole. Admittedly it is rather arrogant to say that and saying it might quite plausibly indicate "sour grapes" on my part, but I have strong doubts that there ever has been anyone who has ever reached such a station. In my opinion it is more likely that assuming the validity of such claims about oneself or others will easily lead one into self-deception and away from the kind of practical experiences that are useful for progress.

My guess is that the journey has always been one of uneven movement. The advanced adept can perform mystically well for hours at a time, and sometimes even days and weeks, and then in the next moment she can make a gaffe as unsightly as the emotional outburst of a five-year-old. These gaffes are painful blessings if registered in awareness and acknowledged, and pathologic when denied and hidden under a cloud of self-deception. The king who is able to notice when his clothing is gone is way ahead in the mystical game.

For me, the consummation of mystical ability does not define a level of mastery which would always reliably allow one to cross the mystical threshold. But the consummation of mystical skill can be usefully, if approximately, defined, as follows: the ability to move to the threshold at will, and to intuitively grasp the know-how that allows one to remain at the place from which one can be taken across and delivered into the ecstatic mystical experience. Consummate skill does not mean one can execute the crossing at will.

How does one know one is approaching a consummate level of mystical skill? It is there when one attains the ability to move to the threshold at will, and realizes a clear grasp of mystical ecstasy when it occurs. You will know it when you get in that neighborhood.

It is both difficult and rewarding to continually keep in mind that in every moment, either ecstasy or the vehicle which delivers one to ecstasy is immediately available. Continually noticing that availability is the only cultivation one may need. There is nowhere else besides right here to find the jewel.

The purpose of meditation and other related cultivation practices is to help the practitioner more deeply and continually realize that there is nothing to do. But one has to reach a certain body-mind disposition in order to attain that realization. And so paradoxically the purpose of practice is to realize why one need not practice, or in fact can do anything else in order to rest in mystical ecstasy.

"Without going out the door she realizes how everything under heaven works; without peeping out the window she knows the way of heaven.
The farther out you travel, the less you understand.
So the adept realizes without traveling, recognizes without viewing, and gets all without trying."
Laozi, chapter 47

When I am particularly resentful, vexed, and sullen, it is useful to slowly say to myself, "Too bad, but for now this is the only place where I can acquire the tools I need to reach that mode of consciousness I want: deliverance. For right now, this is the place to learn the know-how of ecstasy."

Quieting the mind

The quiet mind per se does not liberate. But by quieting my mind through the use of some meditative technique, I will be able to more easily chance upon and then suddenly recognize the psychic dynamics of liberation. Thereafter, I will be able to realize this process more continuously. Once I become thoroughly familiar with the *place* where it happens, I can return there even in the most volatile circumstances.

Many have found liberation only by losing all hope that they would ever find it. It was only through experiencing the hopelessness of all their efforts that they attained the stillness and clarity that were required to see where deliverance was hidden. Their abject surrender caused liberation to reveal its subtle location and its inarticulable methodology. Needless to say, they took a risk; hopelessness is not without danger.

21

Crossing the mystical threshold

"Who would want to get to a place that so
utterly fails to give any promise beyond itself?
Only a person stubborn enough to demand something from nothing. Someone like me."
Carla Ansantina

As I have discussed, there are specific things one
can do to arrive at the threshold of mystical ecstasy.
These things make up what we might call a spiritual
technology. The methods are designed to empty out—to
attain a comprehensive reduction of a mystic's
assumptions about life and her need for rational
meaning.

The mystic arrives at the mystical threshold by
having suspended even her most dearly held beliefs;
she is no longer attached to any of them. In her heart
those beliefs can now be equally assumed to be true or
false. She no longer has the will that anything be this
way or that way. She accepts that anything she believes
about the way things work, or about what value they
have, might be absolutely wrong. The key word is *will*.
She has completely given up her insistence that her
world actually be the way she thinks that it is, or the
way she thinks it should be.

Further, she dismisses any desire for her world to
have a transcendent meaning, nor does she insist it is
meaninglessness. She has reached the extreme of
spiritual poverty. She has given up the natural human

need to be sure that she is in a world where everything is all right.

So here we arrive at the mystical threshold. What happens next? If the mystic is able to avoid falling into a lethal pit of depression or, what is more likely, is able to minimally function despite the depth she has fallen to, there is now only one simple thing to do. The sole task at this point of utter emptiness is to wait and see if the mystical premise is valid. The mystical premise holds that a complete satisfaction with life is immediately available when one becomes completely empty and open to receiving it. The capture of ecstasy depends on doing nothing more than deciding to let it happen and be completely open to the mystical offer, for at least the moment.

And so the mystic, free of everything that had prevented her from doing so, has now arrived here at the place where she can decide to test the mystical calculus. She is empty. Apparently it is this openness of heart which now causes her to begin palpably sensing the presence of something which is waiting at the doorway of her heart. She decides to invite in what is felt there just outside—a mysterious something holding the promise that nothing she ever does or fails to do needs to have any fundamental effect on her immediate happiness. By her free choice she has suspended her will to try to take any rational action to attain happiness. She decides to test out whether or not she can be completely satisfied for no reason, completely fulfilled by doing nothing. Implicitly or explicitly she says "yes" to the outlandish offer.

If she has unequivocally taken that "yes, I will try surrendering" decision, if she incorporates the notion of it within her heart, she will sooner or later be astonished to find out that the mystical premise does indeed work; it demonstrates itself to be effective. Her decision transports her across a mystical threshold and there she will stay in mystical ecstasy as long as she continues to remain free of will and free of reason regarding the happiness project, which is to say as long as she makes no overt attempt to secure happiness. As long as she can avoid the grip of reason and will, for a moment or a month, she will retain a deep sense of well-being, no matter what happens.

Notice there is no Kierkegaardian "leap of faith" here. Soren Kierkegaard advocated taking a religious leap of faith, to boldly accept the faith that somehow beyond reason everything in this world will some day make complete sense. In contrast, the pragmatic apophaticist's decision to be pulled across the mystical threshold (which she can rescind at any time, before or after) need only be a decision taken to test the following proposition: that ridiculous as it may seem, the mystic can enjoy the immediate experience of her being here in this moment, whether or not any other material event happens or not, and whether or not her experience of ecstasy has any ultimate meaning or not. Her decision is *not* based, as that of other mystics is, on a faith that everything will ultimately turn out fine.

The apophatic mystic who has crossed the threshold is free of herself; she no longer requires the world to make any sense. Now she only cares if it works for her, and indeed so far it works better than anything she could have imagined.

And so we see after all the hard work that may be required to get to the threshold, once there, one only needs to make the non-rational decision to accept the unreasonable. One only need say, "Yes, I will try this not sensible stuff."

The promise of mysticism is not something that someone thought up to fill an existential flaw in the Universe. It is a natural phenomenon which mystics have discovered empirically. It is the unimaginable surprise which is found in the fabric of mundane existence, that is to say, within the everyday realm of human experience. The surprise is that one can realize the ability to feel just fine without having any assurance that one will be able to remain fine forever, or even into the next moment. One can attain this ability to be carefree for no reason, right now. If only one's heart can say, "Yes, I will wait and see."

無道 Wu dao: Maintaining the threshold of ecstasy

Mystical ecstasy is reliably maintained by the method called *no method* (wu dao). Wu dao is a secret process which self-discloses its know-how in its own time. It is a self-taught process; it cannot be taught to you by another person. But whoever hangs around long enough in the vast openness and sometimes brutal climate of the void will finally realize how to exercise this hidden method.

Complete deliverance?

Complete mystical attainment is an unlikely proposition, from my limited point of view. However, to the extent that you can graciously surrender and laugh at your spiritual pretensions, however high they might be, you will be able to enjoy yourself nearly all of the time. A smile at yourself will almost always bring good things to you. I have found nothing more enjoyable than sitting in the cauldron of my heart, being wrought by its spontaneous alchemy, while simultaneously engaging the extraordinary wonder of the ordinary world around me.

I should note that a number of mystics cross the threshold and remain in ecstasy for long periods without ever being conscious of saying "yes" and without doing much else than I have described in this chapter. Their surrender to "whatever it is" and the process of being set free is carried out entirely below the level of conscious recognition. These mystics were not trying to do anything, not even trying to surrender, when they crossed the threshold and fell into ecstasy.

22

Rawley Creed's daydream

One day I saw a curtain opening up across the breadth of the sky. A petite redhead dressed in a business suit walked out upon what looked like a cloud and announced, "Okay, that's Act One; you can pick up your stuff and go to the green-room." I looked around and was horrified to discover that I and everyone else in my world had apparently been merely playing roles in a fantasy. In great discomfort I wondered how long this had been going on.

As I left the stage, I was appalled to see the Buddha sitting on a teakwood chair having a cup of green tea with the Inquisitioner who had had Marguerite Porete burned alive in the year 1310. They looked at me and smiled at each other. I awkwardly tried to feign indifference.

Down the hallway I entered a break room. Hitler and St. Francis were laughing hysterically over by the coffee pot. Hitler was describing a day when some lipstick got smeared onto his Iron Cross. I was deeply shaken by the scene, but at the same time I felt something strange and not totally unpleasant happening to me as I became completely unglued. Apparently I was being released from my final thread of mental stability.

I overheard my mind say, "But then what's the point of it all?" as I folded up my costume and held back tears. I tried to get in touch with my feelings, but didn't know whether to laugh or cry.

Then I heard a faraway high-pitched wailing and realized it was my own heart now hopelessly unhinged and distanced from itself. Stricken with an odd mixture of terror and ennui, I stepped into a sunlit alcove where a large greyhound, or someone in a very lifelike costume of one, patted me on the head with its paw. The kindly dog said, "Don't worry, you, your world, everything you were, is ruined. Sift through the ruins and you might now more easily find what cannot be taken from you; that treasure will grant your freedom."

I thanked the dog and wandered down an adjoining hall. I was sickened by the next thought that occurred to me, a threatening premonition of how much more might unravel in Act Two. But after a short time there was another change; it was not too long before my fear started becoming a tiny part in an epic narrative. The show had quickly become one of the most complex and richly compelling dramas I had ever seen; I would not miss the rest of it for the life of me. I put my costume back on and waited impatiently for the curtain to rise.

23

A double-walk

"Being one, he was a student of heaven,
being not one, he was a student of man.
The one in whom neither heaven nor man domi-
nates is called the optimal person."
Zhuangzi, chapter 6

In many mystical traditions the psychic state of *undifferentiated unity* (or *oneness*) is held to be the highest goal of mystical praxis and is deemed to have a fundamental value and, in fact, to have an absolute value. In these traditions, it is frequently described as a *union with the absolute*. Undifferentiated unity is also called by various other terms: *the one, the void, the intuitive, undifferentiated awareness, empty mind*, etc. Within some traditions, the mystic is not aware of anything in this state of awareness; there is no awareness of an ongoing cognitive processes.

An example of *undifferentiated unity* can be seen in the psychic perceptions and responses of a boxer. A skilled boxer's focus of attention is on the total collection and rhythm of his opponent's movements. His attention is undistracted by internal cognitive thoughts or planning. There is little conscious focus on any one detail of what is happening; he sees a right glove immediately coming toward his body but also is aware of a left moving into position to deliver a blow to his head. The boxer is perceiving the totality of his rapidly changing field of awareness and is instantly thoughtlessly (intuitively) processing and responding to the opponent's punches even before he becomes consciously aware of what he has done in response or why he has done it.

In pragmatic apophatic mysticism, as in boxing, this undifferentiated unity is not assumed to have a transcendent value, and it is certainly not privileged with a metaphysical significance. For example, it is not assumed to be a *union with God* (although that possibility is not ruled out). Undifferentiated simply refers to the characteristics of one mode of awareness: a quite effective psychic disposition or posture where one is focused on being present to the entire field of perception.

The vision of separate phenomena

In the mystical literature, the other mode of psychic awareness has been called by one or more of the following: *discriminative thought, cognitive thought, differentiating awareness, conceptual thought, the not one.*

In most mystical traditions this discriminating psychic mode, in which there is cognitive thought occurring, is devalued, taken to have a lesser spiritual value. The *One* is sacred; the *Two* is mundane. This is not the case in the apophaticism of Zhuangzi.

The daoist Zhuangzi describes a bimodal state of awareness as optimal. Here, the differentiated and the undifferentiated occur at the same time. You see an individual head of grain in a field of barley but at the same time you maintain an undifferentiated awareness of the larger field, and indeed of your entire internal and external perceptual field. Another example: You are driving your car intuitively processing and responding to the turns of the road and flow of traffic, and are simultaneously thinking of what you will do at your destination. Both states of awareness are simultaneous and integrated. How well they are integrated may have a large effect on the outcome of the trip.

> "His oneness and his not-oneness are unified."
> *Zhuangzi*, chapter 6

Here, the goal is to blend both modes of mentation so that the adept can most effectively perceive, integrate, and respond to the world he inhabits. Zhuangzi, like our boxer, perceives the field in its totality and intuitively (non-cognitively) processes this information. At the same time he is able to perceive and cognitively separate parts of the field and analytically process some of this information. Discursive thought is occurring under the watchful eye of unified, undifferentiated awareness.

In this daoist approach, neither psychic mode is held to be ideal; however, emphasis is placed on the undifferentiated mode, maintaining an undifferentiated awareness of the whole field.

> "Can you manage the occupations of your soul
> and still hold to the One without fail?"
> *Laozi*, chapter 10

In Zhuangzi the *undifferentiated* is sometimes called "heaven" and the *differentiated* is called "man." The emphasis is on effectively integrating the two.

> "To be skilled in Heavenly affairs and good at
> human ones as well—only the Complete Man can
> encompass that."
> *Zhuangzi*, chapter 24

For the pragmatic apophaticist, the value of the double-view is entirely practical; the aim of integrating the two modes of awareness is simply furthering happiness.

To experience the mystic's double vision, keep your eyes wide open to receive everything in the perceptual field, inside and outside the skin. You are bringing everything together into a focal point of undifferentiated awareness. Continue to maintain that unified vision as you simultaneously watch one or more of the differentiated aspects of the field. Your responses to these aspects are effective because the disposition of the entire field continues to simultaneously inform your decisions.

Humility and Grandiosity

"Scrawny and insignificant, he abides with his fellow humans. Sovereign and powerful, he alone directs the consummation of his transcendence."
Zhuangzi, chapter 5

The mystic, and others as well, may regularly alternate between grandiosity and despair. One sense of my human experience presents me with a vision of complete unification; I have been subsumed into everything. I am it all, and all of it is me. I am the serpent Ouroboros, swallowing the entire world of phenomena, subsuming everything within the vast undifferentiated mystery of my soul. Another sense of my experience estimates my value and significance as equal to or less than a speck of dust. The mystic proceeds effectively because she is simultaneously aware of these two authentic appraisals of her value. Both describe a sincere estimate of her place in her world; she is suspended between the limits of a tiny point of being whose value is highly questionable, and a creature with a potential of reaching unimaginable depths and heights. With both visions continually available, she has been set free to be present in whatever might unfold in the next moment.

24

The void

"The first time I felt that unspeakable joy
was just after recovering from ruining my idea
of myself, my accomplishments, and my abilities.
I had thoroughly spoiled my self-esteem and
was finally free of myself."
Rawley Creed

The void transports us into immediacy; arrival into the nakedness of the moment brings the ability to ecstatically engage the entirety of our world.

The void, one half of Zhuangzi's double-view, is an area within the psyche which is free from my efforts to establish my self-worth, and free from my efforts to establish an ultimate truth. It is free of any assessments of good and evil. Free of any fundamental values. Free of any metaphysical descriptions of experience. Free of any conclusions on immortality or mortality. Free of any affirmations of theism or atheism. Free of any assumptions that life either has meaning or is meaningless. Free of any certainty that one can characterize any experienced phenomenon as being this or that. It is openness to whatever is, and to however what is now might change to something else.

The void repeatedly undercuts the validity of its own foundation. It is merely a tool, a tool absent of any claim to be true or to have future validity; the experience of its effectiveness is expected to be valid only within this immediate moment. The void might have no value, either pragmatic or fundamental, a moment later than now. But for now it has extraordinary practical value to the apophaticist.

The void is emotionally challenging. I will need to entertain the disturbing, plausible thought that I might be ultimately worthless. And all of the information which I have worked hard to gather and integrate, all this spiritual wisdom which I have accumulated about my world, may be grossly mistaken. To the extent that I can continually entertain these self-voiding possibilities, I will be able to maintain and extend the expanse of the void.

My very lack of what I might have wanted to assuredly claim to be true knowledge "will set me free." If I survive exposure to the void, I will experience a visceral sense of ecstasy; I will be free. At this point I will have realized how to love myself and everything else in my world *without needing a reason.*

The void is frightening for the ego. The ego, which functions so well when I have to fix a hole in the roof of the house or sew a button on my shirt, feverishly tries to fill the openness of the psychic void. The ego tries to control and guarantee happiness. When one realizes the nature of the void, the task of rationally constructing a durable happiness becomes quite doubtful. When the ego finally loses all hope of filling the void, darkness comes. If darkness is survived, ecstasy is generated in the wake of the destruction which has occurred.

How does a particular action affect the void?

The criterion for assessing the value of whatever the mystic does and whatever he avoids doing is how it affects the quality and the breadth of the void: acting, cultivating *doing nothing,* praying, imagining, living in devotion, having visions, having sexual intercourse, fasting, fighting, meditating, accepting or rejecting praise or condemnation, talking, remaining silent, etc. On any occasions of these, the simple question might be asked: Is what I am doing (or not doing) increasing or decreasing my vision of the openness of the void? The very same kind of activity can result in either an increase or decrease. However, discerning whether something is decreasing or increasing the void is subtle. We can easily fool ourselves. At times misery can more effectively open the void than prayer or meditation.

Beliefs and disbeliefs also affect the void. The only thing relevant is the pragmatic question: How does this belief or disbelief affect the degree of openness in the void? How is it extending or shrinking the void?

As an example, if your author claims with assurance that he is presenting an authentic spiritual model in this book, he is clumsily trying to fill the void.

Void as a window

It can be useful to think of the void as a window. The void is clear glass that lets you perceive everything in the moment. It is free of thoughts that take you away from this ecstatic immediacy. This look into the richness of the moment amounts to a window cleaning—a suspension (not elimination) of the assumed validity of all that had been gathered by previous views into the perceptual field.

The most entrenched preconceptions are those that dogmatically claim or deny the existence of an afterlife. These speculative views would claim to have established either salvation (immortality) or annihilation (mortality). Because these issues are so dear to the human psyche, they are themes that are hard to release from the mind. But by being harbored there, they fog up the window into the immediate. In other words, they distract one from the ecstatic vision that is available in the moment.

"Attain optimal emptiness."
Laozi, chapter 16

The same void that threatens to render life meaningless is the void that opens one's heart up to a pricelessly auspicious experience: Mystical ecstasy—the escape from the normal limits of the ego.

"I love the void. It gives me nothing and
that nothing takes care of everything.
Nothing always makes me happy."
Carla Ansantina

The void neither promises transcendence nor does it condemn you to the nullity of nihilism. It embraces all possibility. Such is the astonishing wonder of deliverance, the sublime quality of grace.

25

Danger and opportunity

"The Yakut Gavril Alekseyev states that each shaman has a Bird-of-Prey-Mother...
When the soul has reached maturity the bird...
cuts the candidate's body into bits, and distributes
them among the evil spirits of disease and death.
Each spirit devours that part of the body that is
his share; this gives the future shaman power to
cure the corresponding diseases."[1]
                    Mircea Eliade

There are dangers in the cultivation of mystical
ability, and especially in those realizations which result
in wider awareness and possibilities. Cleared of its
structures of meaning, the mind is forced to confront
data which questions the basic values of human
existence. The loss of these carefully maintained
structures can rip an ego apart.

As the mind slows during deep meditation and
gently drifts into a more serene and open state, it loses
the protection of craftily built defense mechanisms.
These devices are used to structure meaning and value
in life, and to keep the mind busy enough so that it does
not stop to question the endurance or value of its
existence. In that time after outdated meanings are
released and before new more effective approaches
have taken root, one can feel adrift with no compass.
An aspirant can lose hope who has not learned that
dryness, instability, and gloom characterize a typical

event in mystical development, and that similar episodes will reoccur.

Depression and despair are not uncommon side effects of intense mystical cultivation. It is an apophatic mistake to declare that nothing should ever be done to treat such depression. It is misleading to claim that since everything is a blessing, one should not seek therapy or medical treatment for depression. Intense depression is dangerous, and can even be fatal. It may be difficult to tell when one has become dangerously depressed and needs medical help. When in doubt, it is best to seek expert advice.

Spiritually speaking, if I purposely inflict pain on myself by not seeking treatment for depression, I am manifesting a willfulness which is not only dangerous, but is also counterproductive to apophatic development. Such willfulness is often a sign of an ego that wants the glory of "going it alone." The problem with that is that there is no glory in apophatic mysticism. If glory is what I want, I best look somewhere else.

If you are depressed but are not suffering serious depression, or if you have already sought medical treatment for depression, it is prudent to get some benefit from the depression. When depressed, one is sometimes able to arrive at insights which one could not obtain elsewhere.

"Oh darkness that guided me! Oh darkness
so much kinder than the dawn!"
San Juan de la Cruz

Depression and profound gloom can uncover some spiritual treasures that are difficult to find anywhere else. Few mystical writers have clearly warned us how treacherous the results of mystical practice can be, nor have they explained how effectively this hazardous negativity can be transmuted into treasure.

The root of spiritual darkness

During the last two centuries a number of great minds have investigated what has been called "existential angst."[2] They tell us that the fundamental root of human anxiety is based in our fear of meaninglessness. The fact of human mortality puts into question virtually all human value systems. One of the major enterprises of religion is to secure meaning for human life. Religions are systems of belief which aim to guarantee a positive and eternal meaning for life.

Herein resides the apophaticist's problem. Fixed beliefs and disbeliefs establish low ceilings on spiritual creativity. Hence, the apophatic practitioner provisionally suspends all beliefs and disbeliefs. But in doing so he exposes himself to morbid doubts; he becomes vulnerable to anxiety over the fundamental meaning and value of his existence.

The emptying experience

"The first lesson I learned took me five years.
The guide I had at that time refused to teach
me anything else until I got it. Finally I got it;
I learned how to feel good about letting myself
feel horrid."
Carla Ansantina

When I provisionally empty out all fixed beliefs, I am emptying out the certitude of those beliefs which had formerly given my life value. This emptying is commonly accompanied by a dreadful affective and viscerally disturbing depression; it can be described psychologically as a plunging fall into hopelessness or at least into an extremely hope-deficient condition. The ailment has been called *spiritual dryness*, an apt description for a condition during which one generally loses interest in things, in particular spiritual themes. As I plunge into this hellish anhedonia, or when I reach the bottom of it, if I am lucky enough to have previously found out how the brutal game works, I know that I will again be confronted by a choice between two alternatives. Each of the options is reasonable.

One option is despair. It makes sense to despair in the face of what appears to be a reality-based hopelessness. And, in fact, to be cleansed of my habit of maintaining fixed systems of beliefs and values, I must recognize that despair would be a perfectly logical option to choose at this point. However, it isn't practical for me to actually choose despair, rational as that option appears to be. If I sense that I am beginning to despair I would probably be foolish not to seek medical attention.

The other option is to not despair but rather push further into the hellish experience. If I have regained enough energy to do it, it is useful to explore the grave dark emptiness which I find surrounding me. I may need the help of a companion to lift my spirits high enough to dare to look into the darkness. When I do begin to explore, my objective is to find out whether or not there indeed is anything useful to find after the mind has lost most of its hope and belief.

If I am fortunate, I will have enough stamina to alchemically process my feelings of overwhelming weakness (see below). Through that work, I then may begin to detect something in the ground of my being that suggests to me there is something useful hidden in this darkness. Although I may have lost all my rational means of establishing a positive self-evaluation, and although I am doubting the value of anything, everything may not have been entirely lost. Gazing into the depths of surrounding darkness, I may catch a small glimmer of insight.

A strange idea may arise from that glimmer: My life might actually have sufficient worth without needing any logical reason for its value. An unseen force in the darkness may propose that an immutable value can be present even where there is no objective evidence of value. If I can trust what I sense there, I may realize that my value has no connection with performing or failing to perform. The glimmer that I see may reveal that I need no excuse for my value other than the simple fact of my existence.

But then I might think of despairing again. Surely the temptation to despair evidences my unredeemable lack of value? But the unseen force next might communicate the notion that there is nothing wrong with despairing. According to this voice, if I do finally end up being completely defeated by despair, I will have done nothing wrong.

To some, the thought of suicide might come to mind, seemingly the ultimate human failure. Thoughts of suicide are a clear indication that one needs expert help. But after seeking appropriate help, one might still dare to challenge the invisible ground of one's being by asking it, "What if I killed myself?" The astonishing reply that some mystics have experienced shoots back like an echo: "If you were forced to make that tragic decision, you still would be loved no less. There is simply nothing you can do that would condemn you."

When this happened to me, after a period of exquisite pain, I began to dimly suspect that I had fallen, not into a pit of hellish finality, but into an amazing state of grace. There in the pit I recognized that I am perfectly fine no matter what I do or don't do, no matter what I feel or don't feel. Somewhat perplexingly, I found that any attempt at self-judgment or guilt was incapacitated by the unrelenting positive force in which I had become immersed. An inexplicable love had emerged from nowhere and had established its ubiquitous presence. I was unable to condemn myself for any imaginable transgression.

Somewhat later, having emerged from the darkness, I noted that this immutable worth which I had found in myself seemed to be present in every other being. I smile as I consider that I might not have become so thoroughly convinced of the plausibility of this unconditional value, if I had been told of it anywhere else apart from that hellish episode of despair.

Today, although I have worked with it for many years, I am still not always certain of the treasure I find in the dark night; at times I still question the validity of my sense of immutable value in all things. I regularly wonder to myself, "Do I actually have anything?" I can feel quite empty at these points.

But this feeling of the void is the root of a thriving apophatic praxis. It helps me realize that I have nothing which I can surely keep. I have nothing for certain but the experience of this moment. To the extent I can arrest my continual temptation to exit from this moment, I will constantly find its naked immediacy to be astonishingly satisfying.

Alchemy: Transmuting negative force

"When the cold brings frost and snow is falling
we realize how the pine and cypress thrive.
The distress I suffered between Zhen and Cai
was a blessing indeed."
Zhuangzi, chapter 27

In the process of spiritual growth, one of the most difficult things to deal with is negative emotion. A sad mood is usually taken as a clear indication of some kind of failure. The practice of internal alchemy utilizes the occurrence of negative feelings as an opportunity to enhance spiritual evolution.

When a dismal feeling or a physical pain is employed as an object of mental focus, this action initiates an internal psychic process. If we intensify and concentrate our visceral awareness on the specific location and quality of the pain or anxiety, rather than intellectually mulling over the ramifications of what is happening, the psyche is able to subconsciously transform the feeling into an energetic force that begins to heal and strengthen psychic stamina. Once the process starts, it is spontaneously guided by its own internal dynamic. This dynamic transmutes the negativity into a force potential, a force which promotes positive transformative growth. The process of transmutation occurs without conscious direction, and in fact it is slowed down if concurrent mental rumination occurs. Internal alchemy, along with other meditative practices, will over a period of time instill a nearly continuous and unshakable sense of underlying well-being.

Various spiritual traditions have complex esoteric manuals outlining these internal alchemical processes, but the process can be learned by working almost exclusively with the resources of one's own mind. This is because internal alchemy is an entirely natural psycho-physical process; it is like bicycle riding. We don't intellectually learn to balance and ride a bicycle; we simply get on and the internal dynamics of our human nature teach us the skill. When we *sit* on the mind, resisting its tendency to ruminate about the grief, and instead let ourselves *feel* what we feel, we begin to spontaneously transmute grief into gold. With protracted effort we learn the art of Zhuangzi: "Making a springtime of every circumstance."

Visualization

"Embrace what the world throws away."
Zhuangzi, chapter 33

To experiment with using visualization to transmute negativity, try the following activity. On a particular day when you're feeling oppression in your head, body, or both, find a place to sit down and focus all awareness on that awful sensation. Then create an abstract image of the feeling as a fiery inferno. The image of the fire is used to kindle a psycho-physiological process in which the images, and all others, will themselves be incinerated. Visualize and then viscerally feel the inferno burning into your heart and refining a quality therein. When refined, this quality will become a stable source of charismatic presence, the presence that allows us to become intimately resonant with other beings during every kind of circumstance.

Long periods of oppression

For a long period of oppression, I suggest that you attempt to alchemically process only small portions of it. For the most part, during such an extended period, you may be better off merely trying to distract yourself with some other kind of enterprise. Take more naps, watch television, or learn to speak Spanish. Keep in mind that processing even a small part of the oppression will bring quite noticeable results. This apophatic work is not a religious mandate; nobody is keeping time or score. If you start to believe that you truly must (should) do as much of this painful processing as you are capable of, as fast as you can, you have probably lost the apophatic path.

Notes:

1. Mircea Eliade: *Shamanism* (London: Routledge and Kegan, 1964).

2. Ernest Becker and the many other authors he cites in his excellent book *The Denial of Death* give us a detailed analysis of existential angst (New York: The Free Press, 1973).

26

Nihilism

Many of us have a continual subconscious fear which William Shakespeare made consciously available to us:

"Life's but a walking shadow, a poor player
That struts and frets his hour upon the stage,
And then is heard no more: it is a tale
Told by an idiot, full of sound and fury,
Signifying nothing."

Macbeth—Act V, Scene 5

Some writers on mysticism are keen to emphasize that the *emptiness* of mysticism does not amount to nihilism. While that may be a fair assumption, such writers may be a bit too quick to dismiss the practical value of entertaining the possibility of nihilism. The plausible characterization of human life as a nihilistic existence is a useful idea for the apophaticist to entertain as a possibility.

Under the threat of nihilism's possible validity, the mystic can reach an optimal degree of spiritual poverty. Through that poverty she notices that if the human situation turned out to be truly nihilistic, there would seemingly be no *reason* to love anything. But that is exactly the kind of love she is aiming to achieve, love which is not shored up by any kind of certainty, love which finds no rational reason and needs none. This is the kind of love she wants because she has found from experience that the most joyful love is one unencumbered by reason. Unconditional love is unlimited by any threat, rational or irrational. This is a rich poverty indeed.

The *threat* of nihilism (which produces the dark night of the soul) is an essential apophatic dynamic. But, unlike the classic existential philosopher, the pragmatic apophaticist does not know that nihilism actually does accurately depict the human's true situation. Unlike those philosophers, the apophaticist does not celebrate the courageous finality with which the existentialist surrenders to meaninglessness. The apophaticist does not know that life is meaningless. Unlike some nihilists, the apophaticist is not trying to outdo the noble heights of religion (belief).

For the apophaticist the only value of nihilism is that it threatens to be true. Other than that, it has no more importance than any other theoretical possibility.

The apophatic alchemist takes the purported, and quite plausible threat, of an ultimate hopelessness of human existence, and pours it with a hundred other beautiful and ugly fragments of her world into a steaming cauldron. There, she forges a love that is undaunted by nihilism. Her recipe has realized the always available raw moment of a love unlimited by any threat or other contingency.

27

Sex and mystical cultivation

Cultivating mystical presence through sexual activity is one way of improving mystical skill. Although it has been condemned from some quarters, and abused by others, sexual techniques have arguably demonstrated their effectiveness in some esoteric communities. My own limited experience with this method has proved useful to my practice.

One of the key dynamics of this method occurs in the period of anticipation before sexual activity. During this period the mind can be readily taught to transfix itself in one-pointed concentrated awareness. In this highly focused phase the mind is free of verbal or imagery content; the central thing one is aware of is the intense visceral feeling associated with sexual anticipation. The transfixing expectation sharpens the acuity of awareness.

The attainment of mind clearing and concurrent hyper-awareness is one aim of the practice. As discussed earlier, the *memory* of the location of this intense presence of mind can be registered and accessed later in order to bring this acutely focused awareness to all of one's other activities, 99% of which remain outside the sexual arena.

The *Zohar*, a work from the Kabbalah mystical tradition, describes this process of sexual cultivation and the subsequent transference of the intense mystical presence to daily life. In the first phase of his devotional practice, the Rabbi cultivates the divine presence during conjugal activity with his wife and *engraves* this presence in awareness. In the second phase, he maintains this intensity of divine presence even when he is apart from his wife. By the sacralization of his conjugal relationship with his wife, the divine presence becomes ubiquitous.[1]

From what I have seen and heard reported, sexual cultivation has many pitfalls and there is no way of reliably vetting trustworthy persons who can teach the practice. But my guess is that two people who have already established an enduring committed relationship can sacralize the sexual aspect of that relationship by developing modes of cultivation under the guidance of their own intuitional wisdom.

In my cultivation of ecstatic ability, I have not yet found it prudent to use any sexual methods which require the participation of another person, and so I have avoided that approach. However, there are sexual cultivation methods, such as visualization exercises, which do not need another person's actual presence or participation.

Both sexual activity and the maintenance of celibacy can become obsessions. Fortunately, there are many other more convenient methods of enhancing mystical skill. If you learn the tricks of the trade, standing in the line at the checkout counter of the grocery store can be as effective as any other method.

Notes:

1. Scholem, Gershom. *Zohar: The Book of Splendor.* (New York: Schocken Books, 1963) pages 10–13.

28

Jesus and Zhuangzi

以道觀之，物無貴賤；以物觀之，自貴而相賤

> "From the view of the dao, creatures are neither
> noble nor mean. But from the view of creatures
> themselves, they see themselves as noble and see
> the others as mean."
>
> *Zhuangzi*, chapter 17

In Zhuangzi, we find the *daoguan* and the *renguan*.
The daoguan is the amoral view (guan) of the dao. In
the dao view nothing is deemed to be either good or
evil; the view is one of a non-discriminate unity. On the
other hand, in the *renguan* (human mind's view), there
are discriminations made. The everyday organization of
human life, especially social interactions, divides things
up into good and bad. For example, law enforcement
translates this notion into legal and illegal. In Zhuangzi,
as the adept perceives, integrates, and responds to her
perceptual field, her process is informed by both views,
the daoguan and the renguan. Her process is an
intuitive integration of both views, the amoral and the
moral.

Amorality, the non-judgmental daoguan, is beauti-
fully demonstrated in the Christian Bible in John,
chapter 8:

1 But Jesus went to the mount of Olives.

2 And early in the morning he came again into the temple, and all the people came to him; and he sat down and taught them.

3 And the scribes and the Pharisees bring to him a woman taken in adultery, and having set her in the midst,

4 they say to him, Teacher, this woman has been taken in the very act, committing adultery.

5 Now in the law Moses has commanded us to stone such; thou therefore, what sayest thou?

6 But this they said proving him, that they might have something to accuse him of. But Jesus, having stooped down, wrote with his finger on the ground.

7 But when they continued asking him, he lifted himself up and said to them, Let him that is without sin among you first cast the stone at her.

8 And again stooping down he wrote on the ground.

9 But they, having heard that, went out one by one beginning from the elder ones until the last; and Jesus was left alone and the woman standing there.

10 And Jesus, lifting himself up and seeing no one but the woman, said to her, Woman, where are those thine accusers? Has no one condemned thee?

11 And she said, No one, sir. And Jesus said to her, Neither do I condemn thee: go, and sin no more.

How exquisite! Informed by an amoral daoguan, Jesus recognizes that if we look from a wide perspective, we find out that we all break rules—we are all similar. We all "sin." He takes this daoguan into consideration as he tells those fellows, "Who is without sin?" But he also recognizes the community and family need for social order, that's why he tells the woman, "Sin no more."[1]

Here in John 8, Jesus is seeing what Zhuangzi calls a *double-view* and is doing what Zhuangzi calls a *double-walk*: "Castigation and favor, benevolence and correctness, the spirit has no use for these. Who besides the adept can make proper use of them?" (*Zhuangzi*, chapter 13)

Notes:

1. The Holy Scriptures.

29

Apophatic bhakti?

"There is something in this place that responds
to prayer and devotion. I don't need to waste any
of my time bothering to ask what it really is."
Carla Ansantina

Gravity works, even though we don't know why.
Prayer works for some of us, even though we don't
know if there is a deliberating external agency who
actually receives the prayer.

At first blush, it would seem that there is no place
for prayer and devotion within a pragmatic apophatic
mysticism. Would you not have to believe in the
existence of that god to whom you say you are devoted?
No, it turns out that belief and disbelief do not have to
determine the efficacy of prayer.

The pragmatic apophatic course is adjusted solely
according to the desired outcome of any practice. That
means that the mystic utilizes whatever is currently
working. If eating pickles works, the mystic eats
pickles. If a disbelief in something is working, that
disbelief is allowed to remain operative as long as it is
useful. If professing a belief in something is currently
obtaining a desired outcome, that belief is maintained
as long as the outcome is produced. And if praying
without holding any belief or disbelief is working, that
practice is provisionally continued.

It appears that what happens during devotional prayer might be generated by a channeling and focusing of emotional energy. During prayer, the expression of emotion may cause changes in the psyche (probably both psychological and neurological changes). The focus of the devotion concentrates consciousness by focusing on a single object, the devotional object.

Prayer examined phenomenologically

When you pray, you externalize an intention. It does not seem to matter whether you have correctly concluded that there actually is a recipient for your prayer. It does not matter, for example, that you might have prayed to a god who does not exist. This is probably because by praying to a perceived external power, you have implicitly recognized that what you want will require that you engage and collaborate with a complex of unidentifiable forces located both within and far beyond your own psyche. Prayer at the phenomenological level can be described as simply a means of making an operative contract with these internal and external forces. When you articulate such a contract, you surrender some of your analytical determination. The surrender of a degree of analytical decision-making allows the intuitive aspect of the psyche to operate more freely.

This psychological and neurological surrender resets and optimizes the resonance among all the forces that are coming to the fore; this enhances the resonance between your psyche and the world it inhabits. This increased resonance allows the inner and outer forces to collaboratively succeed. What they produce might not be exactly what you intended, but it will be auspicious.

Prayer is an intensification of communication between the individual and the dynamic processes within the world this individual inhabits. When the communication is intimate, these dynamics begin to act upon the individual as if they were a mother taking care of her child. Such behavior on the part of these forces may give the impression that it is some kind of god acting. Whether or not the prayer phenomenon demonstrates the existence of a god is of no interest to the apophaticist. He is interested only in the quality of the fruit, not the correct identification of the tree.

30

靜 Jing: Stillness at the center

In the process of psychic transformation, the daoist centerpiece is tranquility (*Jing*). *Jing* is the psychic posture that allows the adept to effectively perceive and engage his world. *Jing* describes a singular calmness that subsumes other concurrent mental processes which are dynamic. *Jing* is not idleness or inertia.

"Thirty spokes come together to make a wheel,
but it is the emptiness that allows it to function
on a cart."
Laozi, chapter 11

Laozi is pointing out that the effectiveness of function in mechanics depends on relationships between solid parts and spaces, specifically on the ability of open sections to receive a part and channel it into effective action.

This is an apt analogy for *Jing*: the coordination of overt activity by a critical psychic area where there is no perceivable movement, like a wheel's center. The overt activity may be physical or mental, but in either case it is coordinated by keeping this key part of the psyche free from detectable (conscious) noise. *Jing* is stillness at the center of activity, a calmness that provides for an effective integration of perception and activity.

"Like the compliance of a whetstone, flawlessly
integrated, moving or still, no mistake is made."
Zhuangzi, chapter 33

It is not only subconscious activity which this calm psychic central ground is integrating. Undistracted by the noise of internal conversations (conscious articulated thinking), the mind's concentrated attention achieves a pristine view of everything within the field of perception, a clear and simultaneous reception of both internal and external information:

"Still water clearly reflects even hairs, so even more does the spiritual essence. The sage sets her heart by this stillness. Thus she mirrors heaven and earth; thus she reflects aspirations of all beings."
Zhuangzi, chapter 13

With clarity of vision and a tranquil conscious mind, there is nothing to interfere with the remarkable capacity of the preconscious mind to effectively process and respond to the complexities of reality. Stilling that critical zone allows the integration of complex combinations of subconscious and conscious inter-activity; the psyche is able to accurately perceive, integrate ("make things one," *Zhuangzi*, chapter 1), and respond coherently to the complex data and distur-bances that occur in the internal and external worlds. Zhuangzi calls this trait "peacefulness in the midst of volatility." (chapter 6)

The primary purpose of *Jing* is not introspection; it is not an attempt to fix the psyche through internal inspection and repair. The mind will spontaneously function effectively if it is freed from superficial worries (and one such worry is an over-preoccupation with self). The focus of *Jing* is rather toward an appreciation for, and intimate engagement of, the world and all its inhabitants:

"With his heart transfixed in stillness, others are moved to cooperate. It is said that his receptive stillness pervades heaven and earth, penetrating all

beings. It is called the joy of the heavens;
this heavenly joy in the heart of the sage
enables him to nurture everyone."
Zhuangzi, chapter 13

Tranquility is the balanced state of a mind that has reached optimum potential.

"Emptied out he is stilled, stilled he is impelled
into action, acting he achieves the optimum."
Zhuangzi, chapter 13

It is functioning with the maximum effectiveness that can be achieved from seamlessly integrating all of the capabilities in its design. When the mind operates at such refined intensity, it effortlessly moves the world around it.

"I cherish tranquility (*Jing*) and the people perfect themselves."
Laozi, chapter 5

Part Two

Pandora's Box

Dear Reader,

I would encourage you to try a nonlinear approach to what follows. Instead of going to the next page, you might "roll the dice" and simply open the book anywhere amid the randomly arranged subjects in this next section. This would be doing the "crooked walk" of Zhuangzi, a way of proceeding which he found to most effectively bring him where he needed to go.

Pandora's Box

"It's the one who has the ability to get it from within herself, whether she is under a big tree or in an empty cave, who gets satisfaction from whatever happens. If she can't get it out of herself, even if she possesses an empire and everyone is her subject, it won't be enough for consummate growth. If a person can get to a point where there is nothing (in particular) that she enjoys, then there will be nothing that she does not enjoy. This is to arrive at optimal enjoyment."

From Section 16 of the *Huainanzi*

∧∧∧∧∧∧∧∧∧∧∧∧∧∧∧∧∧∧∧∧∧∧∧∧∧∧∧∧∧∧∧∧∧∧∧∧∧

To communicate effectively we need to collaborate with each other in a deception. We have to provisionally pretend that we can express clear and reliable ideas. But this façade of reliability and clarity hides an underlying ambiguity which is of equal authenticity. And so finally we must reach toward each other in the darkness. We engage each other with a language that is as honest as we can make it; an honesty that candidly admits to the ambiguity and equivocation which neither of us can ever reduce. While disheartened by our communication deficits, we reach out anyway. We dare to love, despite our inescapable doubts about love. We have found the uncanny authority of unconditional love.

∧∧∧∧∧∧∧∧∧∧∧∧∧∧∧∧∧∧∧∧∧∧∧∧∧∧∧∧∧∧∧∧∧∧∧∧∧

Danger and opportunity

The apophatic mystic does not argue with death. That is why her sense of well-being will remain vulnerable. This is why her sense of freedom and unconditional love remain undauntable.

∧∧∧∧∧∧∧∧∧∧∧∧∧∧∧∧∧∧∧∧∧∧∧∧∧∧∧∧∧∧∧∧∧∧∧∧∧∧

"I can only recommend what an angel told me, 'Put no God before love.' "

Carla Ansantina

∧∧∧∧∧∧∧∧∧∧∧∧∧∧∧∧∧∧∧∧∧∧∧∧∧∧∧∧∧∧∧∧∧∧∧∧∧∧

The richness of spiritual poverty

"The inch-worm moves forward by contracting."

The Book of Changes

Spiritual poverty means owning nothing but immediate experience. The less we try to drag along with us into this moment, the more we will find within it. The more we lose by contracting our egos through spiritual poverty, the more we go forward toward ecstasy.

∧∧∧∧∧∧∧∧∧∧∧∧∧∧∧∧∧∧∧∧∧∧∧∧∧∧∧∧∧∧∧∧∧∧∧∧∧∧

"Blessed are the poor in spirit, for theirs is the kingdom of heaven."

Jesus: Matthew, chapter 5:3

For the mystical adept, material riches are not that difficult to deal with effectively, whether she possesses them or loses them. Far more difficult to root out is the pride that often results from spiritually dramatic experiences.

Saint Paul's and Martin Luther's prescription for "faith not works" can be seen as an expression of a generic universal mystical formula. It tells us that it does not matter what you have done or are doing; the mystical process will proceed auspiciously if, and only if, you are in the requisite mind-body disposition. It is the same advice given by Laozi: "Do nothing."

In my interpretation, *faith* is equivalent to simply being in the ecstatic disposition. It is both where the mystic wants to go and also the way to get there. Works, if rooted in spiritual poverty, can lead one toward ecstasy, but works are also quite effective at leading one's attention away from ecstasy. We lose our poverty when we put too much emphasis on the success of our work.

∧∧∧∧∧∧∧∧∧∧∧∧∧∧∧∧∧∧∧∧∧∧∧∧∧∧∧∧∧∧∧∧

"How difficultly shall those who have riches enter into the kingdom of God; for it is easier for a camel to enter through a needle's eye than for a rich man to enter into the kingdom of God."

Luke, chapter 18:24

Getting one's gold through the eye of the needle will be hard, but not as hard as a proud sense of spiritual accomplishment. Spiritual pride will make it impossible to arrive at the threshold and enter into the mystical disposition.

Looking at that small hole (I use a vision of a pinpoint in a wall rather than a needle's eye) helps you be continually aware of how much baggage you are bringing with you, and how difficult it will be to go in the direction you want carrying all that baggage.

Materially rich baggage is not a big problem, at least not for the god-intoxicated seeker. The thoughts that occupy the mind, particularly thoughts of performance-based value, are the most difficult of the riches to excise in one's attempt to approach the needle's eye. But then this is not an eye that we will have to get completely through; the journey will be quite enjoyable by simply moving toward it.

^^

It is so very hard to get through the eye of that needle Jesus talked about. And when you have written a book purporting to explain how to get through that eye, you have greatly increased the effort you will need. It will be hard to get through if you have to bring that book and your other "important" projects with you.

^^

My two best friends are doubt and failure. These friends humiliate me. And humiliation forms the root of mystical power. As Jesus said, "Lucky are the poor in spirit."

The spiritual poverty that underlies the efficacy of apophaticism necessitates giving up any certainty that the practice itself has any fundamental value. On the other hand, I have found much practical value in it. The practice is a lot of fun most of the time, and has been deeply rewarding to me. But when anything more beyond practical value is claimed for it, its vitality is reduced.

^^

"The sage does not accumulate things. He gives to others and thus enriches himself more. Giving away what he has, he ends up with much more."

Laozi, chapter 81

In the experience of spiritual poverty it is not you, the individual, who becomes worthless. You are as precious as everything else. In spiritual poverty what is found to be worthless is your pretension to own more than your immediate experience. Fully satisfied with immediacy, you will experience the immutable value of your being.

^^

"Become as self-composed as if you were continually offering a sacrifice to the gods of the earth."

Zhuangzi, chapter 17

Here, one sees the relationship between the psychological state the Daoist cultivates and the evolution of the Daoist ethos from the priests and shamans that came before them. The sacred awe with which the Shaman approached the gods speaks of the intimacy the Daoist seeks with "everything under heaven."

^^

天 Tian: Heaven

For Zhuangzi, heaven (tian) was not somewhere to go. It was about being right here in a radically different manner. Tian was not a place but rather a mode of consciousness.

^^

"This is a little strange. You act as if there is something so significant to do that you can forget God while you do it."

Carla Ansantina

^^

Whatever distracts you

A global awareness of and attention to the entire field of the moment's content allows the intuitive processes to effectively proceed and aptly respond to events. Whatever might pull your attention away from a comprehensive awareness of this moment—thoughts of God, the Ultimate, the Absolute, perfection, atheism, truth, enlightenment, mortality, immortality, nihilism, good, evil, safety, danger, etc.—are things that are not allowed to dominate the psyche if mystical intuition is to be effective.

^^

Failing at failure

"Its utter uselessness is the very thing that makes it so useful."

Zhuangzi, chapter 26

There have been a good number of days when I have failed miserably at non-contingency, failed to surrender to circumstances so that I could allow myself to be delivered from all concerns. On these occasions I was holding too tightly on to something. But there is that interesting mystical equation called *successfully failing*. If I can sustain a gentle internal smile of acceptance toward myself when I fail, I will actually be doing quite well. The alternative—failing at failure—is quite painful.

Yet even then there is no need to ever lose all hope; there is always another twist. Failing at failure can potentially be even more liberating. The wretchedly lower you go, if you survive, the freer you are to go higher the next time.

∧∧∧∧∧∧∧∧∧∧∧∧∧∧∧∧∧∧∧∧∧∧∧∧∧∧∧∧∧∧∧∧∧∧

此 Ci: This

The simple pronoun *this* is the term Laozi used to name the agent of his mystical know-how. *Ci* is the experience of holistic presence, the sense of immediacy derived from giving undivided attention to the totality of current internal and external perceptions. It is a surrender to the fullness of the moment. It is *this*.

∧∧∧∧∧∧∧∧∧∧∧∧∧∧∧∧∧∧∧∧∧∧∧∧∧∧∧∧∧∧∧∧∧∧

Vanishing Gods

You have lost even the slightest evidence, concrete or intuitive, that the mystical dynamic exists. Your best guess is that you have been taken for a complete fool. But luckily someone had warned you ahead of time about the *vanishing Gods*. Underlying your miserable condition you begin to notice an unusually calm base of satisfaction.

You patiently wait and happily notice that in spite of your disappointment there is a *whatever-it-is* that does not seem to be disappointed with you. You feel grateful and soon are suddenly struck with such an overwhelming sense of being unconditionally loved by this entity that you are no longer concerned that it might not exist.

^^

The experience of losing everything, or a large quantity of what you had, can be useful in realizing spiritual poverty. On the other hand, pride in having the *status* of one who has lost most of what he had is not helpful in maintaining spiritual poverty. Status is not useful and static mysticism does not work. You might say to the universe, "Look, I gave up almost everything. Does that not make me noteworthy, at least in some small way?" And you may hear the universe gently reply, "No, you have always been and will be, as perfect as everyone else. Your blessing of suffering a big loss should have helped you realize that."

^^

The all-embracing

Angela of Foligno was mystically adept enough to see from a perspective where murder, along with everything else in the universe, is perfectly okay. But she may not have been adept enough to see that being repulsed by murder is also perfectly okay. She apparently did not see that being repulsed by the idea of an unfair God is also okay. The all-embracing embraces everything.

^^

"It seems that where you and I differ the most is that when we have significantly different assumptions about actuality, I think that your assumptions might be right but you think that mine cannot be right. I think you might be right about that."

Rawley Creed

^^

As soon as the mind becomes aware that it exists, it notices its various relationships, it notes individual gains and losses, and guilt arises. To defend myself against guilt, my mind is continually rearranging the furniture of its world so that I will look good and you will look bad. Deliverance (liberation, ecstasy) occurs when I realize that guilt has no coherent or consistent basis; it is at that place that I am able to realize an unconditional fondness for the world and every being in it. It is at that point that I no longer need you to look bad.

^^

For me, what is so powerful in Pema Chödrön's approach is that she is not claiming to present a spiritual path which will culminate in a total solution for every fundamental existential problem. Instead she suggests a flexible course which can richly enhance experience. Like Laozi she is telling us we can "realize that we already have enough to be satisfied." We do not need perfection. She offers a way whose effectiveness is variable but on the whole generously rewarding. Chödrön offers an approach which is pragmatic and largely effective; it is practical liberation, not a perfect metaphysical liberation.

^^

"I avoid recognition whenever feasible, but not out of humility. I just don't want to be seduced from my faith

in nothing. I like being god-intoxicated and I'll pass on
any ecstasy-diluting remedies."

Rawley Creed

∧∧∧∧∧∧∧∧∧∧∧∧∧∧∧∧∧∧∧∧∧∧∧∧∧∧∧∧∧∧∧∧

"Birthdays remind you that the Christmas story is also
about you."

Carla Ansantina

∧∧∧∧∧∧∧∧∧∧∧∧∧∧∧∧∧∧∧∧∧∧∧∧∧∧∧∧∧∧∧∧

Disintegrated awareness

Sometimes a person wants to meditate but can't
quiet her mind enough to do so. And there are times
when a quiet mind is not working satisfactorily. There
is an alternative method which does not require a great
deal of quietness.

Disintegrated awareness is a meditation exercise in
which attention loosely attends to a number of things,
and attending to no one thing in particular. There is an
observation of bits of internal images arraying
themselves in continually disintegrating patterns. The
mind's eye sees these vague images fluctuating in
gently chaotic movements. The viscera detect random,
mild internal pushes and pulls. The eyes are open and
wander aimlessly around the visual field.

In this exercise the cognitive function of the psyche
is scattered about, and thus the psyche is being trained
how to limit the production of coherent concrete
thoughts. As in other forms of meditation, the ability to
subordinate the analytical mode of thinking enhances
the psyche's ability to free up the deeper modes of
psychic functioning. These deeper modes are then
better able to bring rapt attention to the moment of

intimate connection, intimate connection with another individual and/or with the entire perceptual field.

^^^

"Bubble, bubble, toil and trouble."
Macbeth, William Shakespeare

Although I don't think it is wise to look for trouble, it cannot be overstated how effective misery is when applied to internal alchemical processing. As a reminder, each time I notice myself miserable, whether it is for the minute, hour, or several days, I recite Shakespeare's witches' formula. I visualize myself stirring a pot of treasures and traumas bubbling on the fire, fueling and refining the mystical jewel of deliverance. I painfully acknowledge how powerful misery can be. If I am going to feel horrid, I might as well get something out of it.

^^

Dream work

Many of my dreams are useful to me, for example the ones in which I am posturing. These remind me how ingrained my ego perspective is. I find it enjoyable to work on the nearly impossible task of freeing myself from that posturing. The embarrassment of watching myself assume some pose in dreams is useful medicine for this work. The memory of that embarrassment helps me catch myself doing the posturing while I am awake.

^^

Only a God can truly make sense of what It has created. But the rest of us must pretend that we can. We have to find fairness and logic operating in our world. Without the pretense of rationality and order, even the most basic of our daily survival tasks becomes overwhelming.

Attaining a humble clarity reveals to us that the fact of our self-deception is a double-edged sword. Those who are aware of this necessary game of deception are found in one of two groups. They are either the most happy or the most despairing among us. Lucky are those who have learned how to fall in love with a world which has yet to convince them how it can make enough sense.

∧∧∧∧∧∧∧∧∧∧∧∧∧∧∧∧∧∧∧∧∧∧∧∧∧∧∧∧∧∧∧∧∧∧

"One day I lost 80,000 dollars in less than two hours, but I heard a voice telling me there was nothing lost worth grieving. I wondered if the voice was 'The Lord God' who I had read about in the books of the prophets. Indeed, a great peace descended upon me. But to be honest I was still not completely sure if I should believe what this Lord God told me, or get an appointment to see a psychiatrist."

Rawley Creed

∧∧∧∧∧∧∧∧∧∧∧∧∧∧∧∧∧∧∧∧∧∧∧∧∧∧∧∧∧∧∧∧∧∧

Relax, no one is keeping score in heaven or hell. The pragmatic apophatic mystic senses that she fails at nothing essential if she fails at mysticism and returns to a more normal approach to life. But at the moment her curiosity still has the best of her.

∧∧∧∧∧∧∧∧∧∧∧∧∧∧∧∧∧∧∧∧∧∧∧∧∧∧∧∧∧∧∧∧∧∧

A longing for love

The human being sometimes senses an essential aloneness. We can never have each other to the extent that we feel we need to. And we can't possess our world with the intensity it seems to deserve. But ecstatic love frees you to fully love even what you cannot have. The mystic is able to step out of herself and enjoy love far beyond the boundaries set by human limits.

^^

Empty and thusly filled

Ironically, your recognition that it might be likely your experience of transcendence has no metaphysical validity, that it is arguably only an act of the flesh, might sublimely heighten the intensity of the experience. Your breath may be taken away by a gripping visceral sensation as you are stunned by the grace of a singular deliverance which appears to need no logical basis. You have been liberated from both material and theological calculations. Your fondness for the world is released from every contingency; you have been captured by unreasonable love. You have met what some mystics call God; you are free to call it whatever you like.

^^

"Do whatever form of cultivation you enjoy, the more the better. And while you are at it, keep in mind that your activity and what it might bring are quite possibly all meaningless. With the admission of that possibility, your cultivation will be ten times more effective."

Rawley Creed

^^

When you calculate your material and spiritual capital and find that its total actual value has reached the sum of zero, you will find that your heart is then open enough to recognize the presence of what is called *the all-embracing.*

^^

This writer's enthusiasm might at times have an odor of proselytization. This behavior is uncalled for because apophaticism lacks the assurance of an enduring reliability that would make it worthy of recommendation. It is working for me at the moment, but I have no reason to be confident that it will work well for you.

^^

Rawley Creed was asked, "What if it turned out that your compelling interest in other people was merely related to their use as vehicles for your own transformation? What if your God is actually only your morbidly narcissistic self-absorption?"

Creed replied, "Well, I guess you have to work with what you got."

^^

I want to destabilize my idea of a world so that I don't miss seeing anything that I could not have expected.

^^

Don't clutter your heart with hopes and plans. What we now need has already arrived. Allow yourself to indulge in the sheer vitality of this moment.

∧∧∧∧∧∧∧∧∧∧∧∧∧∧∧∧∧∧∧∧∧∧∧∧∧∧∧∧∧∧∧∧∧

When Nietzsche discovered the "death of God," he did not realize that another God was simultaneously born. For he had made the death of God into his own personal God. Trying to make apophaticism into a substitute for God amounts to the same self-deception.

∧∧∧∧∧∧∧∧∧∧∧∧∧∧∧∧∧∧∧∧∧∧∧∧∧∧∧∧∧∧∧∧∧

Mystics do not rise entirely above human emotion where neither love nor hate is finally forsaken. But the mystic's reaction to things is tempered by an intuitive sense for the complementing value of everything. She realizes an all-embracing affection for the world as it shows up in the moment.

∧∧∧∧∧∧∧∧∧∧∧∧∧∧∧∧∧∧∧∧∧∧∧∧∧∧∧∧∧∧∧∧∧

Love is less promising than sacrifice

In terms of spirituality, sacrifice is a means of finally overcoming the human condition and bringing about a resurrection of something greater. In contrast, apophatic love is an embrace and celebration of what is apparently an as-yet-unresolved situation.

Sacrifice instills the hope of a transcendent future. Apophatic love promises nothing beyond now.

∧∧∧∧∧∧∧∧∧∧∧∧∧∧∧∧∧∧∧∧∧∧∧∧∧∧∧∧∧∧∧∧∧

The deeper you want to go, the thicker and harder is the stuff you will have to break through. The deeper you want to go, the more painfully you will have to work at removing and letting go. It would appear to be prudent not to dig too deep. Mystics need to be imprudent.

∧∧∧∧∧∧∧∧∧∧∧∧∧∧∧∧∧∧∧∧∧∧∧∧∧∧∧∧∧∧∧∧∧

When we are work-centered, the work becomes oppressive. When we are centered in the jewel, work is play.

∧∧∧∧∧∧∧∧∧∧∧∧∧∧∧∧∧∧∧∧∧∧∧∧∧∧∧∧∧∧∧∧∧

I appreciate that my current disturbance won't last. But I also don't want to run away from the benefit and the pleasure that is in this pain. Waste not, want not.

∧∧∧∧∧∧∧∧∧∧∧∧∧∧∧∧∧∧∧∧∧∧∧∧∧∧∧∧∧∧∧∧∧

An example of what Sartre calls "bad faith" is me telling you that I have all the answers, and simultaneously being unaware that my statement quite possibly results from a self-deception. Bad faith has been the occupation of many great theologians.

∧∧∧∧∧∧∧∧∧∧∧∧∧∧∧∧∧∧∧∧∧∧∧∧∧∧∧∧∧∧∧∧∧

The spiritual athlete

Material non-contingency (not being affected by material gains and losses) is difficult to achieve. And spiritual non-contingency (being free of the need to be spiritually successful) is nearly impossible.

Surrender is the hardest thing for the athlete. Your love will be sublime if you can be successful at losing.

^^

Terrors and treasures abound just beyond the edge of consciousness. Preemptively befriend all of them and in that way each of them in time will be compelled to deliver you to the jewel of liberation.

^^

Certainty also works

While I have found apophaticism to be spiritually effective, I have also known people who effectively practice certainty. I certainly don't know if one practice may be better than the other.

^^

The dynamics of deliverance

I optimize liberation by clearly recognizing how thin the ground I stand upon is. And I also recognize that there is probably enough support under me to take care of everything that is arriving in this moment.

^^

"I imitate God: I magnanimously smile kindly on my disbelief in God and also on my disbelief in God's absence. I love myself unconditionally, and so I have no problem loving you."

Carla Ansantina

^^

I held myself at arm's length and was repulsed by what I saw. But I was then distracted by giggling and the voices of no one that I could see. Their laughter became uncontrollable as they gasped with impolite glee. Breathlessly they asked me how I had come to judge such a darling little creature so meanly.

^^^^^^^^^^^^^^^^^^^^^^^^^^^^^^^^^^^^^

The existentialist philosopher Jean-Paul Sartre considered the enjoyment of "mundane" activities to have no fundamental value. From the apophatic view it is best not to denigrate "worldly" activities. For this mystic, the very act of a person denigrating activities such as bingo, movies, or golf is the epitome of worldly behavior. It is a behavior which she wants to be free of. If she denigrates the *worldly,* it clearly reveals that she is very much still bound by the world's system of values.

^^^^^^^^^^^^^^^^^^^^^^^^^^^^^^^^^^^^^

Carla Ansantina was asked, "What if a God told you that you were going to Hell, or that there is no Heaven and no Hell, or that everything that exists now will be annihilated?"

Carla said, "That would be fine with me: I have no interest in what happens later; I am only interested in love now."

^^^^^^^^^^^^^^^^^^^^^^^^^^^^^^^^^^^^^

You can be at the center of everything, and you can be that right now. All you need to do is to learn how to be nothing.

^^^^^^^^^^^^^^^^^^^^^^^^^^^^^^^^^^^^^

Over the years I have struggled with great difficulty and recently have been able to obtain a small degree of humility. I am far more humble now than I have ever been. If I am able to go far enough with this, I will finally gain enough humility to realize and humbly admit defeat and accept my intractable arrogance.

^^

The apophatic mystic effectively obviates the disturbing force of death by first of all surrendering to the apparent undeniability and legitimacy of its power. Second, she remains transfixed to the stunning quality of immediacy. And so on a practical level, living entirely in the moment, she reduces the rightful power of death to a continual "not yet."

^^

"The story of Jesus Christ is partly a myth about wanting a God who can experience human despair. In the end, the myth perhaps fails at the human level. Despair is the one thing an all-powerful God cannot do. It can create one, but it cannot become a human being. The failed myth reveals a more powerful myth: the precious miracle of being human."

Rawley Creed

^^

"The problem with many religions is that most people think they need to produce a rational reason for love."

Carla Ansantina

^^

When is love called mystical? Mystical love is love that sees and does not blink.

If it was a God who created mystical love, she did a fine job of it. Mystical love is a love which astonishingly increases in depth and scope even when, and especially when, it is looking into the fearful face of a world that threatens meaninglessness. It is a love which is tenaciously resilient precisely because it has no apparent foundation.

^^^^^^^^^^^^^^^^^^^^^^^^^^^^^^^^^^^^^

My desire is to have a spirit which is both integrated and boundless. That combination usually does not work. But love is a mystery which has no difficulty in joining the two.

^^^^^^^^^^^^^^^^^^^^^^^^^^^^^^^^^^^^^

"Nothing" is something that works well for me. The suspicion of worthlessness can be a quite riveting awakening. I get to immediacy best when I have nothing of purported value inside me to occupy my interest, nothing to prevent me from clearly seeing the arrival of this moment.

I become immediate more easily when I discard my valued collections of supposed wisdom and encounter the immediacy of you.

^^^^^^^^^^^^^^^^^^^^^^^^^^^^^^^^^^^^^

Writing about mysticism

Every word I articulate, especially one that I put down in writing, implies that "it is this way, not that way." Anything which I assert potentially distances me from my reader. Even if I say that I know that I might be wrong, the reader may have good reason to doubt my sincerity.

If I ever meet you face to face, I will try to do better. I will try to forget my ideas and listen to yours. That will be in my self-interest; listening to your view is my only entry to ecstasy.

∧∧∧∧∧∧∧∧∧∧∧∧∧∧∧∧∧∧∧∧∧∧∧∧∧∧∧∧∧∧∧∧∧∧∧∧∧

Having a very big God

When we human beings look for a God, we seek one who can justify our existence and relieve all of our existential anxieties. That is a tall order, and so we usually try to find the biggest God (it may be an idea) we can. But such an endeavor is fraught with difficulty. If I have a triumphalist God, I will be separating myself from those who have lesser Gods, and those who have no God at all. The apophaticist desires not to distance himself from anyone, and so he prefers to entertain, for the moment, whatever kind of God best suits the one with whom he is conversing: a big God, a little one, or none at all.

∧∧∧∧∧∧∧∧∧∧∧∧∧∧∧∧∧∧∧∧∧∧∧∧∧∧∧∧∧∧∧∧∧∧∧∧∧

"If I can't be wrong, I can't be flexible."

Rawley Creed

∧∧∧∧∧∧∧∧∧∧∧∧∧∧∧∧∧∧∧∧∧∧∧∧∧∧∧∧∧∧∧∧∧∧∧∧∧

You can't control the terms of grace's activity. You can't control its direction, content, or velocity. But you can make it happen. Grace has no choice but to happen when you force yourself to allow it to happen.

^^^

The mystic is being embraced by something which is irrevocably beyond his imagination. It is never so close as when he has no idea what it is.

^^^

"You're telling me that you believe in something just because it makes you feel good? Well okay, I don't know of any higher truth than that."

Rawley Creed

^^^

To the degree that you can sense how pathetic your attempts at mystical mastery are, you will be successful. It is not that you should stop your efforts, but simply be able to sense both the irony and the endearing innocence of your struggle.

^^^

If someone tells me that if I don't follow their God I will go to hell, I tell them that I think that could be true. The fact is, I want to stay open and be ready to notice the arrival of things that might even be much stranger than hell.

^^^

I do think theurgy is valid in a certain sense. As soon as I head downstream, the water is forced to move me along.

^^^

There is something, some dynamic at play here, which allows me to enjoy life as it unfolds in this moment, no matter what, if any, ultimate meaning I think that my life might have. There is probably some prime organizing dynamic that permits things to work this way, just as there is probably some primary explanation for gravity. The something is something that I have discovered that I can love, and perhaps it is even more lovable because it apparently will bestow its benefits on us whether we specifically love it or not. If we merely love, it benefits us.

Whatever it is, a personal god or an indifferent natural phenomenon, if we have learned how to work it, it gives its gift unconditionally. Little wonder that some of us are in love with our sense of it, whether it "actually" exists or not, and whether that kind of love makes any sense or not. We feel loved and we respond to the something's love, with love unconditionally.

^^^

"I could not find anything that I wanted to believe, and so I prayed to 'whoever it may concern.' I asked for a religion designed to suit all my needs. It did not take long for an answer. I got this religion where I don't have to believe anything and I get nothing in return for my devotion to it. And this nothing turns out to be everything I need."

Carla Ansantina

^^^

"As I put the beans in my mouth, I looked over at my other arm with dismay. It had stretched far across the face of the Earth, and that hand was snatching my next

145

bite of food from the mouth of an unknown child, sitting out over there under a dust-blown sky."

Rawley Creed

∧∧∧∧∧∧∧∧∧∧∧∧∧∧∧∧∧∧∧∧∧∧∧∧∧∧∧∧∧∧∧∧∧∧∧∧∧∧∧

"Some of your best friends will first appear to you dressed as enemies."

Rawley Creed

∧∧∧∧∧∧∧∧∧∧∧∧∧∧∧∧∧∧∧∧∧∧∧∧∧∧∧∧∧∧∧∧∧∧∧∧∧∧∧

Telling stories that have more creative outcomes

We all struggle with the instability of reality. In daily life I am a constant storyteller, minute by minute my interior ruminations provide a semblance of coherence in my attempt to explain the meaning of what is happening to me. This largely fictionalized linear account of my life gives the chaotic world of circumstance an illusion of predictability, and it allows me to pretend to competence. Some illusion of control is vital to my psychological stability; without some basic stories to patch over large "flaws" in the surrounding chaos, I would suffer madness.

On the other hand, my stories inevitable forecast (cast beforehand) narrowly conceived outcomes. Such a restricted imagination severely limits my potential. If I can rein in this stubborn habit of prematurely editing my ongoing story, the world around me will add rich and unthinkable possibilities to the narrative. If I can allow myself to entertain the possibility of what I can't yet imagine, the results might be quite striking.

∧∧∧∧∧∧∧∧∧∧∧∧∧∧∧∧∧∧∧∧∧∧∧∧∧∧∧∧∧∧∧∧∧∧∧∧∧∧∧

"And I applied my heart to the knowledge of wisdom,
and to the wisdom of madness and folly."

Ecclesiastes 1:17

∧∧∧∧∧∧∧∧∧∧∧∧∧∧∧∧∧∧∧∧∧∧∧∧∧∧∧∧∧∧∧∧∧∧

A delicate existence

One day I had a vision of all the people I know, and
all the ones I don't know, and all of the other beings
living in my world. All of them were cut-out figures
made of colorful tissue paper. I noticed the delicate
contingency of each one, and loved each of them more
than ever before.

∧∧∧∧∧∧∧∧∧∧∧∧∧∧∧∧∧∧∧∧∧∧∧∧∧∧∧∧∧∧∧∧∧∧

Material capital is relatively easy to give up; much
more difficult to surrender is spiritual capital.
Completely divest yourself of faith, hope, and belief.
Also dismiss faithlessness, hopelessness, and disbelief.
Now, with nothing left to show for your lifetime of
noble effort, you stand naked before a threshold.
Thusly clothed you are able to join the poor in spirit
and enter the moment of undiluted love. Here, you will
experience more than you could possibly imagine.

∧∧∧∧∧∧∧∧∧∧∧∧∧∧∧∧∧∧∧∧∧∧∧∧∧∧∧∧∧∧∧∧∧∧

There are a number of spiritual traditions who have
a distinct distaste for the purported existence of the
human self. But even though the self is apparently a
miniscule aspect of everything else that exists, it is
strongly resistant to removal, at least as long as that
which produces the phenomenon of *self* is alive. It
looks to me like as long as that lives, try as one might,
one can no more get rid of it than one can annihilate

the entire universe. Irremovable as it might prove to be, we nevertheless might find exquisitely useful ways to enjoy it. Paradoxically, I enjoy the self best when I don't insist that it exists, and when I don't claim that other folks are wrong who say it really does not exist. It might not really.

∧∧∧∧∧∧∧∧∧∧∧∧∧∧∧∧∧∧∧∧∧∧∧∧∧∧∧∧∧∧∧∧∧∧

"Thou shalt have no other gods before me."

Exodus 20:3

An unconventional perspective offers an alternative to the traditional interpretation of this mystically archetypal phrase from the Judeo-Christian scriptures. For the apophaticist it reveals that one is best to have no agenda, religious or otherwise, which would place itself in front of, and would thereby obscure, the amazing quality of the ordinary now unfolding moment. Let no God obscure your vision of the divine moment opening before you.

∧∧∧∧∧∧∧∧∧∧∧∧∧∧∧∧∧∧∧∧∧∧∧∧∧∧∧∧∧∧∧∧∧∧

We are continually building an imaginary stable existence. We don't like large changes, and we are determined to pretend that we can prevent them.

∧∧∧∧∧∧∧∧∧∧∧∧∧∧∧∧∧∧∧∧∧∧∧∧∧∧∧∧∧∧∧∧∧∧

Why complain? It looks like everything in this world is working the way it is designed to work, and failing to work in exactly the way it is designed to fail.

∧∧∧∧∧∧∧∧∧∧∧∧∧∧∧∧∧∧∧∧∧∧∧∧∧∧∧∧∧∧∧∧∧∧

I agree with the ancient Chinese mystic Zhuangzi that morality is a quite necessary hypocrisy. It allows for stability in the family and community. It can never be coherently universal, but is universally useful.

^^

The human innately seeks physical and emotional comfort, just as the bee seeks honey. Emotional comfort can be obtained from finding, or thinking one can find out, how things "really are." By determining certain unchanging fundamental principles, one can attempt to carefully regulate life and give meaning to one's existence. Traditional religion provides this. And even the untraditional *perennial philosophy* and the *mono-myth* provide such a framework.

But there is another choice: One can find surprising emotional comfort solely within the nakedness of this now unfolding moment. Each moment brings changes, sometimes revolutionary changes, but one can notice that so far each moment has also brought everything one has needed to maintain a deep sense of well-being (ecstasy.) Each moment seems able to provide a sense of nearly complete satisfaction, a love for one's world just the way it is now unfolding.

This uncanny sense of well-being seems not to depend on any kind of finally settled knowledge about anything. In fact the love of one's world and the ability to intimately engage other beings in this world seem to grow greater to the degree that what had been one's settled knowledge becomes quite unsettled. As Laozi says, "To learn is to add to one's store each day. To apply the dao is to subtract from it each day." (chapter 48)

^^

Watch for and engage periods of emotional disorder, and especially those when your luck has turned from disorder to complete turmoil. Such a disturbance can provide a fine wroughting of the soul. Don't ruminate; don't move away from yourself; stand in the center of that fire and feel the heat permeating your body and soul. There is no stronger power you can enlist for transformation.

∧∧∧∧∧∧∧∧∧∧∧∧∧∧∧∧∧∧∧∧∧∧∧∧∧∧∧∧∧∧∧∧∧∧∧∧∧∧

I am not interested in expressing my skepticism toward your opinions. What interests me is the root of my own skepticism. I am skeptical of my opinion of your opinions.

∧∧∧∧∧∧∧∧∧∧∧∧∧∧∧∧∧∧∧∧∧∧∧∧∧∧∧∧∧∧∧∧∧∧∧∧∧∧

Fear of reductionism

In the spiritual literature it is common to find vehement defensiveness toward scientific reductionism. Reductionist theorists would reduce all spiritual phenomena to psycho-biological artifacts. The pragmatic apophatic mystic has no interest in defending mysticism against this reductionism. For him, mysticism "is what it is, whatever that is."

If mystical phenomena can be fully accounted for by reductionist theory, so be it. If mysticism amounts to nothing beyond mere neurological matrixes and psychological complexes, well that is just fine with the pragmatic apophaticist. He has no stake in an ultimate validation of his experience. He has no defenses and nothing to defend. This mystic is simply in love with the immediate experience of his world. The fruit of this moment is something for him to enjoy, not something he wishes to authenticate. He has found the unspeakable pleasure of spiritual poverty, and so there is nothing else of interest left to consider.

∧∧∧∧∧∧∧∧∧∧∧∧∧∧∧∧∧∧∧∧∧∧∧∧∧∧∧∧∧∧∧∧∧

To play the mystical game needs an open-heart and a flexible organization of mental and physical facilities. It is a tricky game to win. To be successful you need to recognize that the idea of winning is just as foolish as the idea of losing.

∧∧∧∧∧∧∧∧∧∧∧∧∧∧∧∧∧∧∧∧∧∧∧∧∧∧∧∧∧∧∧∧∧

When you find yourself wired into a manic state of hyperarousal, force each movement of your body and inner mind to proceed with extreme slowness. When your core speed is optimally retarded, you will meet what the mystics used to call God.

∧∧∧∧∧∧∧∧∧∧∧∧∧∧∧∧∧∧∧∧∧∧∧∧∧∧∧∧∧∧∧∧∧

Hitting the spiritual wall

"Satisfied with success and satisfied with utter failure."
Zhuangzi, chapter 30

Hitting the spiritual wall may last for an hour, several days, even months. In some cases this condition has led to the end of a life. What follows is one account of hitting the wall.

But before I describe my experience of the wall, I would like to again remind the reader that I don't take my mystical experiences to be normative. I don't claim that every mystic, or every apophatic mystic, goes through cycles of spiritual brightness and darkness. As far as I know, there may be those of you who have reached a point where everything is eternally joyful. I am but one practitioner. Your decision as to what applies to you is, from my point of view, your sovereign judgment to make.

One day I find myself emotionally unable to generate enough desire to work on writing this book, and I become quite dissatisfied with this inability. And then I realize how much my recent happiness has been dependent on this writing. Now this makes me extremely dissatisfied; I am faced with a cruel irony. I have become attached to writing a book, one of whose major themes is the optimal elimination of attachments.

There is only one way out of this trap and I don't know if I can pull it off. My release will come only if and when I can realize one of the mystic's paradoxical abilities: satisfaction with dissatisfaction. Talk is cheap. Will I be able to walk the walk? And what can I do in the meantime while I remain miserably unable to walk it?

Since I am currently stuck in dissatisfaction, being pragmatic, I might as well see what is going on in this dismal state. Is there anything here I might make use of? If I am going to be vexed, I might as well get some benefit from the painful sting of it.

I notice that in this current state of dissatisfaction I am finding it hard to believe that something, indeed anything, had previously satisfied me and, even more incredulous, had satisfied me extremely. I ask myself what possibly could have given me reason to have been so well pleased. To my chagrin, I am unable to come up with anything. I can think of no justification for my previous over-the-top enjoyment of life.

Ah ha! Herein lays the clue this fool has been looking for. I was so well satisfied before, precisely because there was no reason for it; it depended on nothing that can be established by reason. At this point I make a guess: I figure that when and if I am able to recover that reasonless sense of well-being, I will probably become just as unreasonably satisfied as before, and probably more so.

Whether writing a book or trying to get a better bowling score, it is good not to get too serious about your quest; the most enduring happiness is found in a different place.

∧∧∧∧∧∧∧∧∧∧∧∧∧∧∧∧∧∧∧∧∧∧∧∧∧∧∧∧∧∧∧∧∧

Some say that striving is spiritually counterproductive. I think striving is quite all right. The trick is to strive to go nowhere, to strive to stay right here.

∧∧∧∧∧∧∧∧∧∧∧∧∧∧∧∧∧∧∧∧∧∧∧∧∧∧∧∧∧∧∧∧∧

In practical terms, that is to say, for what is happening right now, mortality and immortality are both fantasy. Apparently there is no one who knows the exact nature or endurance of this human experience. For all we know it might be like the story of Jesus—you die only to find out later that you could not have actually died, for you are God.

∧∧∧∧∧∧∧∧∧∧∧∧∧∧∧∧∧∧∧∧∧∧∧∧∧∧∧∧∧∧∧∧∧

A paradox: the mystic's acceptance of all things importantly includes accepting as valid the view of others who sincerely find many things in their world completely unacceptable.

It is an amazing grace which fails to solve the human being's existential dread, and despite that failure instills an effortless unconditional love and sense of well-being.

∧∧∧∧∧∧∧∧∧∧∧∧∧∧∧∧∧∧∧∧∧∧∧∧∧∧∧∧∧∧∧∧∧

The power to certify truth

What makes it difficult to maintain an attitude of radical receptivity is that we human beings are innately afraid of losing what little power we seem to have. We would like some control against the overwhelming forces that appear to surround us. We commonly and mistakenly think we can get some control over our world by exercising the power to decide what is true about it. Zhuangzi was less interested in what is true, and more interested in the dynamics and benefits of effective human relationships.

The question of power lurks at the foundation of all relationships. Zhuangzi surrenders his natural urge to claim the power to decide what is true. He relinquishes any authority to control the terms of a discourse. He is partial to the view that it will be more advantageous to all involved if he collaborates with others, rather than trying to control others with his own assertions of truth. In such a discourse, "truth" for him becomes one of the issues to be decided *during*, not before, the collaborative process.

Zhuangzi avoids injuring his own well-being by not attempting to assume a unilateral power to decide what is true.

∧∧∧∧∧∧∧∧∧∧∧∧∧∧∧∧∧∧∧∧∧∧∧∧∧∧∧∧∧∧∧∧∧

For me, the whole apophatic game* is aimed at increasing personal satisfaction by means of increasing mystical efficacy. I cultivate mystical efficacy simply because it has, up until the present moment, brought me that satisfaction. If, a moment from now, this mystical paradigm fails, I will probably look for something else. But up to now, it has worked satisfactorily.

I do not aim for, nor expect to reach, any kind of perfection. I suspect that if I believed that perfection can be obtained such a belief would amount to what Sartre calls "bad faith." On the other hand, I do intend to enjoy the game as much as possible for as long as it lasts.

*Note: I use the term "game" advisedly. If anyone is certain that apophaticism is fundamentally more important than a game, I suspect that they might not be able to play this game well.

∧∧∧∧∧∧∧∧∧∧∧∧∧∧∧∧∧∧∧∧∧∧∧∧∧∧∧∧∧∧∧∧∧∧

Don't always trust the mystic's reports

The reports of a mystic are not entirely trustworthy. He is apt to include erroneous material when writing about his subject. He has often had a number of quite dramatic experiences, and so he may vehemently and sincerely insist that the occurrence of these experiences is exclusively associated with the particular circumstances under which they occurred. If he is a member of a particular religion, he may be tempted to believe that his experience demonstrates that only his religion can provide authentic mystical experiences. If he is an atheist, he may claim that it is the only authentic basis of mystical practice. It is best to be free to find your own prejudices.

^^^^^^^^^^^^^^^^^^^^^^^^^^^^^^^^^^^^^^^

Astonishment

We go to a circus, a movie, or sporting event to enjoy being surprised by unusual skills and other stimulating phenomena. The mystical vision opens us to a perspective where we can be astonished by each ordinary moment of experience; we are able to perceive a sublimely numinous thread of surprise as again and again it weaves another coincidence of challenge and opportunity. We catch glimpses of its full radiance as it sews an intricately designed fabric from the random-ness of fate. We become both the audience and the part of the event itself; we are witness to a continuing drama that pervades our perceptual field. I myself am able to see it now and then; I have never seen a spectacle anything like it.

^^^^^^^^^^^^^^^^^^^^^^^^^^^^^^^^^^^^^^^

Opportunities to treasure

Do you feel in an especially ugly mood today? And are feeling even uglier because there is actually nothing materially awry? Are you so impotently miserable that you can't even get angry at yourself or—what's worse—at anybody else?

Well then, if it doesn't kill you, this is your lucky day. There is no more forceful psychic energy than that produced by a tenaciously vexing misery. A misery without cause and without heroes. A misery that you can't write home about.

Dive deeply into this stuff; let it wash over you and suffuse every cell in your body. This power will transmute your soul's energy like nothing can. This kind of pathological despondency is not that easy to find, and so remember to celebrate and painfully enjoy the thought of your unimaginably good fortune this day.

You don't need to thank any gods for it. You probably deserve all the credit for generating such extravagantly beneficial misery.

^^

"Although you can fit a small thing within a big thing, it still can be lost there. But were you to keep the entire world stored within your world, there could be no loss. This not-lose-able is an attribute that is found within all things; it is their immutable quality."

Zhuangzi, chapter 6

^^

Spiritual sovereignty

"By using it (dao) its pivot becomes manifest. Amid the volatility of circumstances, there is no event one cannot effectively respond to."

From the *Huainanzi*

When attentiveness rules the psyche, it is in a condition that is called "being at the pivot." At the pivot, one's fundamental level of satisfaction is entirely under one's control. If one can remain at the pivot, all events and circumstances are intuitively leveraged auspiciously. This mode of consciousness is called "non-contingent contentment." Here, no material event can impinge on one's psychic equilibrium. Here, one achieves spiritual sovereignty.

^^^

On the other side of the mystical threshold is a space that is conceptually impoverished. At first glance it seems as though there is nothing here. Then after a persistent waiting, a fullness is sensed within both mind and bone. In this "empty fullness" the perplexed heart paradoxically grasps the certainty of having returned to its home. A resplendent and yet sober luminosity pervades the psychic field.

^^^

The *perennial philosophy*

Unlike the perennialists, I don't know that there is one "normative" mystical landscape, a single set of authentic mystical dynamics that underlies all genuine mystical paths. Holding or rejecting such a view are both positions that would restrict the openness of apophatic engagement. The religious fundamentalist and the perennialist reject the other's point of view. The apophaticist finds no proof that either position is wrong and rejects neither.

The apophaticist is continually prepared to suspect her motives for favoring one paradigm over another. She is aware that the human ego favors the *truth* of whatever has brought compelling results, especially if this truth has now become *her* way.

^^^

It is tricky for the mystic to work diligently at a task that discounts conventional values, and yet not privilege her work over the value of the conventional goals which hold interest and value for others. The task of the apophaticist is to fulfill both of two conflicting aims. She is taking on a huge and difficult endeavor and yet must stay extremely small if she is to succeed at it. She will have to defeat pride and somehow not become too proud of doing so.

∧∧∧∧∧∧∧∧∧∧∧∧∧∧∧∧∧∧∧∧∧∧∧∧∧∧∧∧∧∧∧∧

If I provide a great help for another person, it won't hurt me to feel good about it. But doing what I did will not increase my mystical vision. It won't deliver me. It is not the good I do for you which will deliver me. It is what I avoid doing inside my head that delivers.

∧∧∧∧∧∧∧∧∧∧∧∧∧∧∧∧∧∧∧∧∧∧∧∧∧∧∧∧∧∧∧∧

Despair is fitting at times

Can you appreciate how fitting despair can be? It is one of a number of plausible responses to the human situation. If I cannot appreciate the rationale of despair, I won't attain a viewpoint that will enable me to enjoy the vast scope and richness of life. And I will find it difficult to communicate with someone who is undergoing despair. Understanding the reasonableness of another person's despair, and honoring its possible validity, is an experience of priceless value.

∧∧∧∧∧∧∧∧∧∧∧∧∧∧∧∧∧∧∧∧∧∧∧∧∧∧∧∧∧∧∧∧

The sovereign soul

When the sense of a need to protect self-esteem has been greatly diminished, one's presence to the surrounding world reaches a greater intimacy.

Zhuangzi says that the sage "does not move until pushed." For a mystic, at all times and places, the direction and time to proceed are indicated by a palpable visceral impulse. The mystic has a clear sense of this signal arriving from an inner psychic guide whose presence is subtly perceived but whose directives are unmistakable. This inner ruler is referred to variously in Lao-Zhuang tradition as the "spirit castle," the "inner mind," the "One," etc. In neo-Confucianism the same dynamic is described by the phrase "let unity be the ruler."

The intellect is usually in the service of the forces that protect self-image. These emotionally charged forces have been trained by the ego to deal with its perceived threats. The forces react autonomously to any ego-image threatening stimulus. Their dynamic reactive pattern is intellectually and emotionally embedded deeply within the psyche. The work of mysticism is to transcend these powerful forces and transfer the leadership of the psyche from fear-based forces to an entity that is free of the need to protect self-image. The task is to re-school the intellect, to teach it a more effective basis of self-value.

The transfer of power to the above-mentioned inner ruler is not intended to obliterate the sense of a self, but to eliminate the deeply entrenched need to protect self-image.

Transformation is the process of giving the intuition sovereignty over one's being, which then allows effective interaction with the larger surrounding reality. When one's sense of a need to protect self-esteem has been diminished, one's sense of presence to the surrounding world reaches maximum intensity. Sovereignty is automatically installed (awakened) during the completion of psychic transformation. Many of the external forces which had previously presented threats are then seen as presenting opportunities for gainful interaction and collaboration. One is liberated from the rule of the ego and is able to reach full human potential.

∧∧∧∧∧∧∧∧∧∧∧∧∧∧∧∧∧∧∧∧∧∧∧∧∧∧∧∧∧∧∧∧∧∧

Aloof and intimate

To achieve deliverance, the ability to love unconditionally, the mystic remains aloof from the conventional values which his neighbor would impose upon him. And at the same time, he finds a ground of emotional intimacy by appreciating that his neighbor's existential situation and desire to thrive are identical to his own. During each encounter with a potentially adversarial neighbor, the unconscious work of an intuitive calculus is able to harmonize what would appear to be two irreconcilable aims.

∧∧∧∧∧∧∧∧∧∧∧∧∧∧∧∧∧∧∧∧∧∧∧∧∧∧∧∧∧∧∧∧∧∧

"Reverently (*Jing*) compose yourself within, and let this diffuse outward to other beings."
Zhuangzi, chapter 23

∧∧∧∧∧∧∧∧∧∧∧∧∧∧∧∧∧∧∧∧∧∧∧∧∧∧∧∧∧∧∧∧∧∧

"Make a springtime of every circumstance."
Zhuangzi, chapter 5

This is realizing how to absorb the power within and effectively respond to the creative freedom which inhabits every moment, the pleasant ones, as well as the catastrophic ones.

∧∧∧∧∧∧∧∧∧∧∧∧∧∧∧∧∧∧∧∧∧∧∧∧∧∧∧∧∧∧∧∧∧∧

The Great Mother

Apophatic mysticism is an esoteric discipline. In fact it is so abstruse that a writer can only recite the most elementary lessons of the practice. For anything more advanced, the would-be apophatist must go directly to the apophatic source. This source, the master teacher, is embodied in the form of a relationship: the relationship between the individual psyche (body and mind) and the world it inhabits.

This interaction, properly cultivated, will systematically teach you all the mysteries of apophaticism. The inner voice of this relationship will speak to you directly as if it were an actual individual.

Cultivate this dynamic relationship, and at a certain critical threshold you will be viscerally gripped by the experience of the Great Mother.

Let no one suggest that they can explain the radiant profundity which is found there at the nexus of the apophatic relationship, at that perpetually gracious and indulgent source which has been aptly called the Great Mother.

^^

"The work of the mystic is to intimately engage unseen forces, not to believe in their existence."

Rawley Creed

^^

As the mind takes in the written word, it is constantly trying to help the writer construct a firm conclusion. Useful apophatic literature does not conclude anything. If it is good, rather than specifying, it performs. It performs an opening to the mystical landscape, none of which can be put into words. As soon as I finalize a thought, I block that opening.

^^

How do you know if you have found the thread of the mystical path?

If you have found a thread of something which seems compelling but is so subtle that you can't find the words to express what it is, follow that thread.

If the thread begins to wander so enigmatically that you think that no one outside of yourself will ever be able to authenticate the validity of your experience, you have undoubtedly obtained a grasp on the thread.

If you begin to have grave doubts about whether mysticism has any real value or not, and yet you are also beginning to find a way to make a sincere friend of every doubt and embrace each of them as allies, you are moving closer to the heart of the practice.

If you are becoming more at ease with the inexplicable mysteries of life and no longer find yourself caring whether you are on a genuine mystical path or are simply practicing self-delusion, you are making excellent progress.

If you are finding fewer things that are able to irritate you each day, you are going in the right direction. You are right on course if you are finding yourself seldom bored and, when you are bored or irritated, are able to apply the negative valence of those emotions to further a positive alchemical transformation.

And if you start to care less about whether you even make any further spiritual progress beyond this modest point where you are right now, if you are beginning to realize that you are perfectly fine with all your unseemly flaws, beginning to feel loved by the ground of your being for no reason at all, then you are indeed exactly where you need to be on this mystical thread.

This condition is called "Still have far to go but have already arrived." Here is probably as far as anyone needs to get; even the sages seek no treasure beyond this one.

∧∧∧∧∧∧∧∧∧∧∧∧∧∧∧∧∧∧∧∧∧∧∧∧∧∧∧∧∧∧∧∧

You will remain on disturbingly shaky ground until you find out why you don't need to be on stable ground.

∧∧∧∧∧∧∧∧∧∧∧∧∧∧∧∧∧∧∧∧∧∧∧∧∧∧∧∧∧∧∧∧

The agent of deliverance

It is only the quality of the ongoing process which has the capacity to deliver. Whatever is manifested by the process, no matter how spectacular, it has no power to liberate. The process of deliverance stays on course as long as there is a continual surrender of each of its manifestations and a continual embrace of immediacy.

Continued deliverance is provided by merely watching the process of the now unfolding. As long as you store nothing, you continue to be free. Zhuangzi's directive to the ego: "Respond but do not store." (chapter 7)

∧∧∧∧∧∧∧∧∧∧∧∧∧∧∧∧∧∧∧∧∧∧∧∧∧∧∧∧∧∧∧∧

When you step outside the lifetime of values you have carefully collected, you encounter great danger and unimaginable opportunity.

∧∧∧∧∧∧∧∧∧∧∧∧∧∧∧∧∧∧∧∧∧∧∧∧∧∧∧∧∧∧∧∧∧∧∧

The mystic has desire, but the thrust of her desire is objectless and she lacks a *specific* agenda. She desires to embody a mystical dynamic which lets her rest in a state of well-being, no matter what she gains or loses.

∧∧∧∧∧∧∧∧∧∧∧∧∧∧∧∧∧∧∧∧∧∧∧∧∧∧∧∧∧∧∧∧∧∧∧

"Merge the dust."
Laozi, chapter 56

"The cloud of unknowing" refers to the same archetypal mode of consciousness which Laozi called "merging the dust." With its undifferentiated awareness, the cloud brings you to the mystical threshold. On the other side of the threshold you will be able to intimately engage separate beings and simultaneously engage the inseparable unity of immediacy.

∧∧∧∧∧∧∧∧∧∧∧∧∧∧∧∧∧∧∧∧∧∧∧∧∧∧∧∧∧∧∧∧∧∧∧

I usually support you whether or not I have any interest in what you are doing. You have my support because giving it to you allows me to approach that in which I am intensely interested: the treasure that lies just behind the veil of appearances. I honestly don't know if I would be so interested in what you are doing if I did not require your collaboration for what I am intent upon.

∧∧∧∧∧∧∧∧∧∧∧∧∧∧∧∧∧∧∧∧∧∧∧∧∧∧∧∧∧∧∧∧∧∧∧

If you can seamlessly insert yourself into a situation, it is more likely your presence will have the potential to improve it.

∧∧∧∧∧∧∧∧∧∧∧∧∧∧∧∧∧∧∧∧∧∧∧∧∧∧∧∧∧∧∧∧∧∧∧∧∧∧

I am a spiritual athlete, and the use of that term betrays my arrogance. I can't get rid of that arrogance but must find a way of limiting its powerful ability to ruin my performance. My first step will be admitting to my lack of humility.

∧∧∧∧∧∧∧∧∧∧∧∧∧∧∧∧∧∧∧∧∧∧∧∧∧∧∧∧∧∧∧∧∧∧∧∧∧∧

"Anyone who intends to follow a spiritual path and thinks that she is not doing something for herself has fallen off that path."

Rawley Creed

∧∧∧∧∧∧∧∧∧∧∧∧∧∧∧∧∧∧∧∧∧∧∧∧∧∧∧∧∧∧∧∧∧∧∧∧∧∧

In the midst of everyday life we can stay tuned into the mystical jewel. If we are tuned in we have access to a great wealth of information and to an uncanny ability to integrate and respond to that data. If we are tuned in, although we cannot *see* any of this unconscious processing, we can get a clear sense of what it is telling us about the gestalt. That clear sense can greatly inform and therefore optimize our decisions. This is commonly called "going with a gut feeling."

∧∧∧∧∧∧∧∧∧∧∧∧∧∧∧∧∧∧∧∧∧∧∧∧∧∧∧∧∧∧∧∧∧∧∧∧∧∧

Apophatic liberation

In apophatic liberation one is not freed from "the sting of death" in the manner that St. Paul meant it.

Instead one is freed from the ability of death to disturb one while one is still alive. Apophatic praxis does not free one from history, from the normal trajectory of a human life. But one is freed from the overwhelming weight of history. Its weight is astonishingly reduced, and this is accomplished without an explainable cause. The sense one gets is that no rational cause is needed for this release, nor would one be believable.

∧∧∧∧∧∧∧∧∧∧∧∧∧∧∧∧∧∧∧∧∧∧∧∧∧∧∧∧∧∧∧∧∧∧∧∧∧

The jewel of unconditional love works best when you don't try to prove the reasonableness of its existence.

∧∧∧∧∧∧∧∧∧∧∧∧∧∧∧∧∧∧∧∧∧∧∧∧∧∧∧∧∧∧∧∧∧∧∧∧∧

The more you shrink, the more you can enjoy life. Shrinking your ego includes shrinking your Gods. That includes the Godly idea that there are no Gods. Shrink whatever you believe, and whatever you doubt, and you will find much more in this moment than what you could ever guess is here.

∧∧∧∧∧∧∧∧∧∧∧∧∧∧∧∧∧∧∧∧∧∧∧∧∧∧∧∧∧∧∧∧∧∧∧∧∧

"I love you because we are one." Another approach: "I love you even though you are probably not me by any reckoning."

∧∧∧∧∧∧∧∧∧∧∧∧∧∧∧∧∧∧∧∧∧∧∧∧∧∧∧∧∧∧∧∧∧∧∧∧∧

"Love arises... simply from my nature."
Zhuangzi, chapter 25

Unconditional love trumps meaning and reason. This is not to assert that one can obtain no meaning or value for existence. It is to say that unconditional love is free from the need to be certain about those things. This is a freedom to love without yet having found a metaphysical rational for love. Here, there is no "I should love." One loves unconditionally simply for the pleasure of it.

∧∧

I like to keep the dark side about an inch away from my heart, ready to pounce on me whenever I try to get more out of life beyond the glorious wonder of the ordinary moment.

∧∧

Death and its brother Meaninglessness

Ecstasy is a hair's breadth away from meaninglessness. And when we attempt to gain security by calculating some kind of rational meaning for our existence, we move farther away from ecstasy, farther away from that amazing love that is free of all conditions.

Openness is the philosopher's stone for the pragmatic apophaticist. The inconvenient aspect about openness is that to be optimally open one needs to be open to everything, and this includes perhaps the most powerful force that haunts the human soul: the thought of death and the meaninglessness that death seems to entail.

Death is brushed off rather easily in many religious and mystical texts. Good solutions are many. But death is only part of the fundamental fear; it is the surface of a deeper concern. The underlying darkness of death contains the threat of meaninglessness. Death is a harbinger of this fear.

A nearly universal angst is the worry that the fact of death will demonstrate the plausibility that human existence is meaninglessness. That possibility is the mystic's most challenging opponent. If one becomes convinced of ultimate meaninglessness, it may extinguish the heart's vitality. On the other hand, burying the fear with some form of psychological or religious denial will often only give it a greater power to disturb the heart. Entertaining the possibility of meaninglessness in full conscious awareness, as one of a number of possible outcomes for human existence, can become one of the mystic's greatest friends.

Entertaining the notion of meaninglessness without being torn apart and thrown into despair is an unhinging and humbling experience, a risky endeavor. But with the apophaticist's lack of interest in anything other than unconditional love, there is no choice but to take that risk. No effort needs to be wasted proving the life has meaning.

In practice, within the experience of unspeakable love, one cares about nothing else; one cares not about life, death, mortality, immortality, meaning, or meaninglessness. Since love has arisen within a realm which holds the possibilities of any of these outcomes, the mystic is thankful for all of them. She does not try to escape death; she sanctifies it and every other possibility that the next moment may hold for her.

And so my suggestion, if you dare: As much as possible, don't lose touch with the quite plausible notion that the fundamental value of the mystical experience, and life itself, might be zero. On one hand this thought can lead into a dangerous despair. On the other hand it is potentially liberating. It allows you to not depend on anything for your well-being except what is available in this moment. If you are able to extract the mystical know-how that can be found in this moment, it will facilitate a deep plunge into the mystery and stunning depths where love becomes completely unbound from the paltry limits of reason. There, love is set free of both rational and irrational fear.

∧∧∧∧∧∧∧∧∧∧∧∧∧∧∧∧∧∧∧∧∧∧∧∧∧∧∧∧∧∧∧∧∧

A practical thing that is most difficult to remember is the continual availability of divine presence.

When I am standing in the cash-only express line at the grocery store and am proud that my nine items are three short of the limit, and two people ahead of me is a rather large woman writing a check with a screaming child in her arms, and I am sure she has at least two dozen items, I best be aware that I have just entered the Inner Sanctum. I am right there where the full presence of the unspeakable is manifest. With the ability to seek nothing beyond the moment, I realize what is already everywhere. As Jacob said, "Surely the LORD is in this place; and I knew it not." Genesis 28:16, KJV

∧∧∧∧∧∧∧∧∧∧∧∧∧∧∧∧∧∧∧∧∧∧∧∧∧∧∧∧∧∧∧∧∧

Drugs

With drugs one might get a taste of the inner radiance of this world. But to regularly experience this glow, to be able to access the sacred ground, I must train my heart to consume each moment of awareness. I need to perceive and digest the freshness of the world as artlessly and accurately as I did when I was a child. Then I will realize the thrill of perceiving the rich essence of the human journey, whether I am watching a sunset or noticing the eye-catching glitter of a candy-wrapper in the litter of a street. An ability to do this without drugs increases the expanse of mystical access. It allows me to be fully awake in both the divine and mundane world, and to enjoy the astonishing unity of the two.

^ ^

According to the myth, the will to understand got the human beings kicked out of paradise. According to the medieval mystics, surrendering the will to understand gets you back in.

^ ^

As soon as I point a critical finger at someone else, I lose the root of my power. I am not saying that the other person is not wrong in some of these cases. I am saying that it does not serve my purpose to be interested in resolving the question in either their favor or in mine.

^ ^

To attain an intimate communion with a person who is in the dying process, one is best to honor two aspects of the situation: One is the apparently irrevocable tragedy of death. Two is the remarkable moment of this life which is able to subsume everything that is here now. No matter what happens later, "The kingdom of heaven is now."

^ ^

Who is he?

Residing within the heart of the mystic is a kindly indulgent observer of the array of internal voices. This is the watcher who listens to all of them; each of them is given a seat at the table. None is told to go away. The voices heard vary from the sublime to the ignominious; there is the lover, the fool, the cynic, the optimist, the rancorous, the generous, the unforgiving, the doubter, the believer, the narcissist, the extrovert, the coward, the nihilist, the compassionate, the despicable, the serious, the vain, the self-righteous, the sociopath, the saint, the selfish, the magnanimous, the atheist, the violent, the meek, the capricious, the arrogant, and the humble.

The heart of the mystic respectfully listens to the claims and counterclaims of each of these conflicting internal voices and calmly referees the discourse. The refereeing is sub-verbal; the referee's voice is sensed but not heard. The gathering and integration of all the voices to produce an auspicious outcome is also a silent intuitive process, much too complex for discursive analysis.

As the mystic heart listens to itself, it can simultaneously hear the diverse assertions of the outside world; it listens to the outsider with the same loving indulgence it bestows on each member of its own internal unruly menagerie. And so the mystic is able to receive every other being with artless grace, with a graciousness attainable only by one who has recognized he can't be sure who or what he is made of.

It seems that to be free of myself and meet you completely, I need to appreciate that I don't know exactly which of my voices I am.

The Jester

Reflecting on the landscape of total psyche facilities, one might picture a large table in the middle of the psyche with different characters seated around it. Characters whose personalities are much like those I just described in the preceding section.

I think one of the most essential ones to be given a place at this table is the Jester. If I can never laugh at and doubt the value of my entire spiritual enterprise, there is likely something seriously wrong with my approach.

The Jester adds a powerful emotional valence to the skeptic's purely intellectual proposition that "I might quite possibly be wrong." Mocking my claims to correctness threatens the ego at this deeper, emotional level, and thus cleans out my pretensions closer to the place where they are rooted, at the source of my emotional sense of well-being. If I can root out my pretensions there, and survive the purgation, my sense of well-being will no longer depend on my intractable need to think of myself as wise.

The Jester can insure that I reach optimal spiritual poverty. I will not let him rule the psyche, but neither should I allow his voice to be quashed.

After the Jester has crushed, at least in theory, my entire spiritual project, and if I survive the decimation, I will be in a void which is free of almost everything. This void is a place where I will be in the best position to locate unconditional love. This love is not conditioned on proving the truth, or the sensibility, of anything.

Zhuangzi was one of the few writers in the history of wisdom literature who considered the utility of being able to risk mocking everything we believe, and everything we think we have learned that purports to constitute wisdom.

However, he was not a simply negative skeptic like Ecclesiastes. Zhuangzi figured you could enjoy life both when you took it seriously and when you did not. He did not make the Jester into an absolute.

The Jester helps me realize that I have not and might never be able to escape the *pleasure principle*. I will probably not be able to prove that I am a creature who is any nobler than a bee going for honey. The Jester dares to assert that although I may develop ingenious methods of obtaining pleasure, it is doubtful that I can make a fundamental change that will qualitatively differentiate me from other beings. I have learned ways to quantitatively deepen pleasure and make it more enduring, but this does not guarantee that my pleasure-seeking is more noble, of a higher fundamental value or purpose, than that of the hedonist.

But what is glorious is that with the Jester's revelation of my apparently inescapable parity with all other creatures, I am released from expending any more energy to maintain a self-deception, and am now freed to seek the most pleasure. The most pleasure for me is found in unconditional love. Unconditional love needs no proof; I don't have to repress my worries about being a fool.

However

For the work of the Jester to be effective, it needs to be limited to a self-mocking, not a mocking of the other person. The Jester mocks my temptation to think I can be certain about the value and course of my life. But the Jester also mocks any temptation I might have to think that you, the other person, cannot be certain of these things. I don't allow my Jester to operate outside its bailiwick; its jestering is only useful inside of me. Taking others as seriously as they want to be taken is essential to intimacy, essential for the generation of my own mystical ecstasy. I would be foolish for calling someone else a fool.

∧∧∧∧∧∧∧∧∧∧∧∧∧∧∧∧∧∧∧∧∧∧∧∧∧∧∧∧∧∧∧∧∧∧∧∧∧

"Coalescing and shattering generate a completion."
Zhuangzi, chapter 26

Within the subconscious mind, a complete disintegration and remixing, a disordering and reordering of the perceived world, are continually occurring, moment to moment. Nothing is fixed in this hidden landscape, and so the picture is always new. Unless it is placed in a straitjacket and safely tied down, the human animal cannot survive for long with this full view of its internal and external world's volatility, chaos, and naked wonder.

Most of us do survive because we have a conscious mind capable of continually constructing an orderly view and a linear narrative for our changing experience. In many cases this ordering and arranging is so well done that creativity, forgiveness, and hence contextual flexibility are nearly eliminated. Life becomes impoverished, adversarial, and burdensome.

The mystic has learned to be simultaneously in touch with the dynamic phenomena generated by both the subconscious and the conscious mind. She is able to serenely ride a whirling torrent of possibility.

∧∧∧∧∧∧∧∧∧∧∧∧∧∧∧∧∧∧∧∧∧∧∧∧∧∧∧∧∧∧∧∧∧∧

The analogy of a wave in the ocean has been used to describe the relationship of the individual to the All. It is said the individual wave does not actually exist; it is only an aspect of the ocean, and so it has no need to fear its potential non-existence. My experience is something different from that picture.

My report so far is that there is a part of me that has a tragic sense of its mortality. This would be the wave's sense of itself existing as an individual in some fashion. And there is another part of me that lives in the ecstatic moment where its love and its sense of love are untouched by any future contingency, unaffected by any concern whether the concern is rational or not. It is a love which seems based beyond me and yet it also pervades me. In the analogy, this would be an ocean's sense of itself.

I don't privilege either view—the wave nor the ocean. I grant legitimacy to both of them. Both of them seem to speak with an authentic voice within me. I don't count on defeating death's sting. So far I have gotten along with it well through the use of a strange mystical calculus: the all-embracing quality of unconditional love.

Self-deception is a possibility, but that possibility has no practical meaning for me. Mistaken or not, I can only act on what I experience to be good for me. I can only report on my sense of the texture of the wave and the ocean that washes over my small spot in the cosmic flow.

^^

When we pray, we pretend to a wider perspective. If our pretence is sincere enough, it will result in the arising of a powerful phenomenon. It is not that there is something verifiably real out there to pray to; it is that you more intensely experience whatever is actually there.

^^

Seeking to gain my own advantage, I try to reduce pride as much as I can. But even if I reduce pride to laughter, I will not have eliminated it. For then pride will simply become proud of me for reducing it to laughter.

^^

I once had a dramatic experience that might be called a realization of mystical unity. But I don't think that that rarified experience needs to be identified as an occurrence of metaphysical unity. I think it was simply the fruit of fully experiencing the mystical mode of awareness for the first time.

Mystical integration is more often a subtle and deep sense of well-being that can be accessed in the best, the most terrifying, and the most mundane of circumstances. A sense of everyday paradise as I wait, for instance, in a crawling line of traffic on the freeway. Find it in the most mundane, the most unremarkable, and then after a while, you will begin to be able to find it everywhere.

^^

"Thou shalt not desire thy neighbour's wife."
Exodus 20:17

Worse than coveting your neighbor's wife is coveting your own ideological possessions. Want nothing to be neither this way nor that, need nothing to be a final truth, and you will get way more than you will ever need to be content.

∧∧∧∧∧∧∧∧∧∧∧∧∧∧∧∧∧∧∧∧∧∧∧∧∧∧∧∧∧∧∧∧∧∧∧∧∧

"Le mieux est l'ennemi du bien." (The perfect is the enemy of the good.)

Voltaire

We apophaticists don't want liberation from everything that is not okay. We want liberation from needing everything to be okay. We don't want perfection. We want to realize how to feel astonishing well without ever realizing perfection.

∧∧∧∧∧∧∧∧∧∧∧∧∧∧∧∧∧∧∧∧∧∧∧∧∧∧∧∧∧∧∧∧∧∧∧∧∧

"There is nothing worse than not realizing one already has enough to be content."

Laozi, chapter 46

I suspect the desire for, and the belief in, the possibility of a final perfection results in self-deception. It is liberating to realize that imperfection is more than enough to allow for great happiness.

∧∧∧∧∧∧∧∧∧∧∧∧∧∧∧∧∧∧∧∧∧∧∧∧∧∧∧∧∧∧∧∧∧∧∧∧∧

A world that can become nearly completely serviceable

Some say that the world is perfect; these folks claim that the only thing we need to do is to realize its perfection.

I once met a woman and her child who was in a sickle-cell anemia crisis. I watched and listened to him screaming in pain as she held him, a pain which his mother told me had been with him most of the days of his short life. And so I am reluctant to say that this world we live in is perfect.

A more modest proposal is to say that if you have lived long enough, you may have been lucky enough to learn how to realize and apply many of life's underlying spiritual dynamics. If so, you have learned how to take virtually anything that happens to you and have it favorably applied to your situation. You who are lucky will have learned how to be quite content in the face of either good fortune or disaster.

You will not have found a perfect world, but rather one that is usually serviceable for your needs. It will meet almost all of your desires, even as it fails to meet the needs of many others. It is useful not to try to find reasons that justify that failure.

∧∧∧∧∧∧∧∧∧∧∧∧∧∧∧∧∧∧∧∧∧∧∧∧∧∧∧∧∧∧∧∧∧∧∧∧∧

Apophatic practice does not eliminate existential fear and angst. Instead it applies the energy produced from fear and anxiety to generate an intuitive non-rational process which transmutes this negative energy into ecstasy.

∧∧∧∧∧∧∧∧∧∧∧∧∧∧∧∧∧∧∧∧∧∧∧∧∧∧∧∧∧∧∧∧∧∧∧∧∧

Don't think you can't influence grace. Modesty inevitably causes the arrival of grace. It is only the form in which grace arrives that cannot be made subject to one's designs.

∧∧∧

Another interview with Rawley Creed

Interviewer: "You describe this non-dependent affection, or love, as arising naturally. I am not sure then how it fits in with man's ultimate purpose?"

Creed: "Actually it does not fit. If it has another purpose, it is not love."

∧∧∧

"The love that Marguerite Porete speaks of is not the love of human beings.... it is only known in our absence."

Carolyn Biagi

∧∧∧

When I get a glimpse of mystical vision, my gaze reveals a landscape that appears to go far beyond anything I can imagine. When this happens, I have an impulse driven by existential angst which moves me to narrow this frighteningly large expanse. Besides trying to narrow my own expanse, I will quite often try to narrow yours.

This is what I do when I say (or imply): I am right and you (the other person) are wrong. I reduce the vast possibilities of my experience.

On the other hand if I assume that you might be right, I greatly increase my own expanse. This is what Zhuangzi called moving "out beyond the six directions." (chapter 7)

∧∧∧∧∧∧∧∧∧∧∧∧∧∧∧∧∧∧∧∧∧∧∧∧∧∧∧∧∧∧∧∧∧∧∧∧∧

"The truth that sets us free" is a rather inconvenient truth. For there are no words to tell us what it is, no words to explain how it could possibly be true.

∧∧∧∧∧∧∧∧∧∧∧∧∧∧∧∧∧∧∧∧∧∧∧∧∧∧∧∧∧∧∧∧∧∧∧∧∧

"On the big rock-candy mountain"

Have you been to the land where everything is all right? The climate there is superb and the food is pretty good. Both love and hatred are all right there. Even things which will never be all right anywhere or any time are all right there.

∧∧∧∧∧∧∧∧∧∧∧∧∧∧∧∧∧∧∧∧∧∧∧∧∧∧∧∧∧∧∧∧∧∧∧∧∧

Tian Qi was holding a feast for a thousand guests. Fish and geese were being served at the head table. Tian looked at the fare and sighed as he said, "Heaven is so indulgent to humans! For our use it generated the five grains and gave birth to the fish and fowl!"

The guests all responded their echoing approval. But a Mr. Bao's twelve-year-old son stepped forward from the group and said, "Sir, what you say is mistaken; all the kinds of beings of heaven and earth are the same as humans. No species is intrinsically precious or mean. It is simply a matter of size, cunning, or strength that lets one dominate the others, that lets one eat the others.

"It is not that one particular being is born designated for another's use. Humans catch what is suitable to eat, and eat it. But can we take that to mean that heaven created them specifically for man's benefit? Furthermore, mosquitoes and gnats bit his skin; tigers and wolves eat his flesh. But we don't assume that heaven created man for the good of the mosquitoes and gnats or to provide meat for the tigers and wolves."

Liezi, chapter 8

∧∧∧∧∧∧∧∧∧∧∧∧∧∧∧∧∧∧∧∧∧∧∧∧∧∧∧∧∧∧∧∧∧∧∧∧∧∧∧

Mystical power

"A man lived by the sea. Every day he would go to the shore and hundreds of seagulls would come to stroll with him. One day his father said, 'I hear that all the seagulls come to roam with you. Catch some and bring them to me so I can play with them.'

"The next day he went to the shore but seagulls would not land."

Liezi, chapter 2

∧∧∧∧∧∧∧∧∧∧∧∧∧∧∧∧∧∧∧∧∧∧∧∧∧∧∧∧∧∧∧∧∧∧∧∧∧∧∧

Something in the ground of your being loves you unconditionally. If you wait at least until your patience becomes painful, sooner or later, it will find you and show you this love.

∧∧∧∧∧∧∧∧∧∧∧∧∧∧∧∧∧∧∧∧∧∧∧∧∧∧∧∧∧∧∧∧∧∧∧∧∧∧∧

Free of me: Not burdened by self-worth

The enhancement and maintenance of a positive self-image are normal healthy human concerns. However, it is worth noticing that we implicitly or explicitly calculate our value by making comparisons with someone or something else. We spend more time and energy pursuing this aim than we are usually aware of. In contrast to this normal human behavior,

Zhuangzi says that the adept is "without significance." He has no interest in establishing his worth. He has found something much more compelling in the immediacy of the moment, and his fascination with this dynamic has caused a complete loss of interest in even the question of his fundamental value. He does not want to be burdened by concerns with establishing his self-worth because these calculations waste energy and impede his ability to step outside of himself into the richness of spiritual immediacy. This immediacy lies intimately close to, but just outside, normal self-awareness.

It is not that he feels worthless; it is that the adept does not sense that he has or needs any comparative value. Some folks call this "free of me."

^^^

I don't take my values or the issue of my self-esteem seriously. I am not actually that interested in the values of my inner world. I am primarily interested in going out to your world and meeting you there. And so I take your values and whatever value you place on your self-esteem quite seriously.

^^^

The Trickster

Even when I am asserting the depth of my stupidity, my ego-bound trickster is fully operative within me. It is, as you might guess, actually claiming to have achieved an incredibly profound wisdom as evidenced by how stupid I have confessed to be.

^^^

When one of his disciples harshly criticized those who worshiped clay idols, Ramakrishna took exception. He noted that it was the intensity of the idol worshippers' devotion to their practice that was the only issue of relevance, not the precision of their metaphysics.

The act of devotion (Bhakti), no matter how flawed its purported metaphysical basis is, can be more useful than an inspiring tract or discussion of a mystical topic. An example of devotion is the gratitude expressed while one is suffering from spiritual and/or physical misery. One might usefully reflect on a quite common experience, the so-called dark night of the soul.

Imagine the following: I am devoted to this dynamic something and honesty forces me to recognize that it is obviously integral to the misery which I am now experiencing. That which loves me is in some manner complicit with whatever is inflicting this terrible distress upon me! By experiencing the puzzling and painfully acknowledged proximity of my suffering with the object of my devotion, I can easily generate an emotional intensity of a far greater order than what I could get from any intellectual discussion of mysticism. The consequent psychic transformation will be substantial.

Here, I am suggesting that the purportedly spiritually naïve person may at times experience the fundamental authenticity of mystical dynamics much more effectively than the person who has a conceptually clear and coherent mystical model.

^^^

Purporting to have a triumphant God or method, or demonstrating my superior courage by claiming to have no God or method—these are both distractions for the apophatic mystic.

∧∧∧∧∧∧∧∧∧∧∧∧∧∧∧∧∧∧∧∧∧∧∧∧∧∧∧∧∧∧∧∧∧∧∧∧∧

One achieves optimal apophatic integration and ecstatic deliverance, not by transcending incompleteness, but rather by embracing, incorporating, and enjoying what might be an irredeemable incompleteness.

∧∧∧∧∧∧∧∧∧∧∧∧∧∧∧∧∧∧∧∧∧∧∧∧∧∧∧∧∧∧∧∧∧∧∧∧∧

An imprudent dose of the divine

I express my desire to become closer to the jewel. I imprudently ask for an undiluted dose. The jewel says, okay, then I will clean out everything that keeps you apart from me. And then I gasp as I wonder why I suddenly end up in a place of utter despair. If I survive that and continue to wait patiently in dysphoria, I finally come to experience a peace and joy that I could not have imagined. This risky exchange of joy and misery happens over and over again, the spiritual landscape of deliverance expanding after each round.

In my case I cannot weigh the risks prudently, after listening to my heart carefully, and I cannot find enough reason not to risk everything. But I would not dare to advise others to take such chances. I think it is best for every person to follow their own inner wisdom. We learn from each other, but the master teacher for each of us sits within our own hearts. Our own internal risk-manager will tell us how much risk to take on, if we listen well.

∧∧∧∧∧∧∧∧∧∧∧∧∧∧∧∧∧∧∧∧∧∧∧∧∧∧∧∧∧∧∧∧∧∧∧∧∧

I don't recognize beforehand that the following is what I am trying to do each time: I am trying to grasp the jewel for keeps. That is why I continue to lose my grip on it. I will do much better when I learn to enjoy it for the moment.

∧∧

自化 Zi hua: Self-directed transformation

The ancient daoists who wrote about self-generated transformation were the first to identify and name this psycho-physical dynamic, one that is similar to what 2000 years later would be called *autopoiesis* by some scientists. This is the ability of an organism to thrive and enhance its own well-being under the guidance of an internally operative dynamic.

∧∧

The benefits of hell

Is your mind currently confronted by an inescapable flow of ideologically vacant and conceptually impoverished images? Sit with as much ease as you can muster with this tasteless fare and its equally tenacious brothers, ennui and stagnation. There is nothing that will deliver you so swiftly to the jewel of liberation than this miserable vehicle you are now riding in. Notice and be grateful that you are graciously excused for your lack of any sincere gratitude for this gift. Don't let your heart be corrupted and distracted by indulging in guilt. Don't let yourself become proud of your despair. The only thing you need to do here is watch and wait. It isn't going to be as bad as you think. Soon it will not be as painful as it is now. Before too long you will be happier than you can imagine about what you found out while you were in hell.

∧∧

What helps when I am in the pit is having an understanding person listen to me. Someone who values what I am saying but at the same time does not encourage me to be a drama queen. A delicate balance.

If such a person is not around, I try to relax into the unpleasantness (or worse) of the experience. I try to remember there is nothing I have to do but wait. I try to remember it is perfectly fine to feel miserable for a time, while also remembering not to become proud of my misery.

I try to recognize the benefits of spiritual poverty without squandering my poverty by playing the martyr. I try to remember to laugh at myself.

∧∧

There are those who experience the mystical disposition as a compelling, unmatched, and extremely liberating "whatever it is." And I think there are others who think it is also that which solves with finality all of the essential dilemmas of human existence. It is probably good to think of it whichever way works better for you.

∧∧

The moonlight reveals a rat scampering into a broken pipe. There is a subtle shift in my awareness and then I discover a sublime pleasure in this quite unremarkable moment. The rat has awakened me again to the extraordinary quality of every ordinary moment.

∧∧

I am a technician, not a metaphysician. I can give you some ideas of how your world might work better for you. But I can't tell you what your world really is, or how you *should* respond to it.

∧∧

Most religions and metaphysical models are presented by authorities who express no doubt that they know what is ultimately good for everybody. I think that any of them might be right. I am willing to express what I think is probably good for me. But I would be hard-pressed to even guess what is good for you. I have found no basis for ascertaining that your beliefs, whatever they may be, are either correct or incorrect, either ultimately useful or not.

∧∧

I got up late and irritable that day. The sun was coming in to annoy my eyes. But it was only when I burned the toast that I finally discovered and got rid of that insidious idea that had been plaguing me for three or four days. I had again slipped into unconsciously harboring that charming but laughable belief that I had a clear idea what life was about and what was really important to do. The ruined toast had freed me again, at least for a little while. Such brief periods of respite from myself are exquisite pleasures, much better, for instance, than eating chocolate or doing a number of other things which I don't need to mention here.

Martin Buber states that Hasidism, in contrast to Christianity, works for the sake of the world, not for the individual's salvation. (*The Way of Man and Ten Rungs*, Martin Buber, pages 30–31)

On my path, which I do not consider to be higher or lower than any other path, I do not attempt to stop behaving in my own self-interest. I suspect that any attempt to do so will result in a self-deception. My attempt to overcome my mind's impoverished idea of self-interest is simply an attempt to obtain a greater self-benefit. My interest in escaping my narrowly limiting self-perspective, and thusly being better able to listen to and appreciate your concerns, is a desire of mine that greatly benefits me. My aims are not as noble as those of Martin Buber, assuming that nobility is a reliably identifiable value.

"Why do I subordinate my agenda? It is simply to get more for myself."

Laozi, chapter 7

∧∧∧∧∧∧∧∧∧∧∧∧∧∧∧∧∧∧∧∧∧∧∧∧∧∧∧∧∧∧∧∧∧∧∧∧

自正 The spontaneous generation of wisdom

The mind, if left to its own devices, so narrowly conceives of self-interest that it behaves in a manner that is actually counterproductive to the interests of the self. This deficit cannot be analytically corrected.

But by simply carefully observing your mind, you may effortlessly cause it to behave with a wisdom that is far greater than anything that can be contrived by its intellectual capacity. If we can allow grace to emerge, the mind can act with an amazing grace.

^^^

The cultivation of mystical ability is best aimed at getting closer to the threshold. This is something that can systematically be done. On the other hand, crossing the mystical threshold is something that cannot be systematically done; it has to be finessed.

^^^

The work of mystical cultivation is paradoxical. You work in order to tune in to that mode of awareness where one can clearly apprehend that there has never been any work that had to be done. When you see that there is no imperative to do any material or spiritual work, you have arrived, even if your arrival lasts only for a moment. This sense of nothing to do forms the basis of mystical non-contingency and the all-embracing mystical heart. The more you are able to maintain that sense of done-ness and arrival, the better your work will be.

^^^

"I have a dedicated religious practice, a practice not hampered by religious beliefs."

Rawley Creed

^^^

Riveted and still at ease

While in the mystical disposition, attention is riveted to the immediacy of the moment. But this is an unusual riveting. There is no effort being expended; the sense you have is one of relaxed alertness and easy flow.

∧∧

I can't see behind the veil; I can't know what it is that is there. But I can grasp it and learn how to use it well.

∧∧

The idea of a God and the idea of there being no God are both sacred ideas. And when you are in love with everything, even nothing is sacred.

∧∧

Apophatic ecstasy is not noetic in the sense of "Now I know what life really means," or "Now I know what is really essential," or "Now I know what is right and wrong." It is noetic only with regard to gaining a know-how. Through ecstasy, I learn how to obtain a compelling sense of non-contingency, a nearly complete deliverance from anxiety and fear.

∧∧

"My friend and I argued vehemently about politics for many years until we finally realized that we were actually in total agreement. We recognized that we each agreed that the other one's position was totally idiotic. After that, there was nothing left to disagree about."

John Coscia

∧∧

Apophatic prayer

If she prays, the apophaticist is not necessarily convinced that she is actually getting in touch with a

God, for it might be that no God exists. Instead she is getting in touch with an unseen dynamic. She is attempting to realize deliverance. She knows that deliverance exists because she has had occasions to experience it before.

∧∧∧∧∧∧∧∧∧∧∧∧∧∧∧∧∧∧∧∧∧∧∧∧∧∧∧∧∧∧∧∧∧∧∧

Nearly insolvent

Stay as close as you safely can to the edge of spiritual insolvency. That edge of vulnerability is where spiritual poverty abides; the source of apophatic ecstasy arises at that hazardous location.

∧∧∧∧∧∧∧∧∧∧∧∧∧∧∧∧∧∧∧∧∧∧∧∧∧∧∧∧∧∧∧∧∧∧∧

Although the mystical sense of well-being is usually unshakable, its unshakability paradoxically depends on vulnerability. The adept responds with equanimity to the most shocking of events. But he realizes that it would only take a slight change in perspective and all of his ability would be lost in a flash. As long as he is able to stay in touch with his vulnerability, he will remain unshakable.

∧∧∧∧∧∧∧∧∧∧∧∧∧∧∧∧∧∧∧∧∧∧∧∧∧∧∧∧∧∧∧∧∧∧∧

To help attain spiritual poverty, it may occasionally be useful to entertain the following idea: It could be that those people who are the most anxious and fearful are the ones who most clearly see a profound gravity in the human condition. Perhaps most of the rest of us are lucky for our ignorance and/or denial of the situation. Am I spiritually poor enough to imagine even a non-apophatic perspective?

∧∧

It is not only that I had to go down into the pit of hell to learn how to do what I am able to do. I have had to always stay a hair's breadth away from that pit in order to retain the skill I learned there.

∧∧

There are mystical traditions in which the adept is called a "master," and this master is said to have attained an ability that is invincible. In apophatic mysticism the key dynamic is spiritual poverty. The durability of the deliverance which one has been able to attain depends on the degree to which one has realized and appreciated how thin and fragile the attainment continually remains.

∧∧

How do I feel when I am alone and nothing interesting seems to be happening? Do I feel distressingly impoverished? In that impoverishment lies the secret of apophatic ecstasy.

∧∧

Dejamiento: Spiritual poverty

Many of us will fail at mysticism because we intensely fear failure. I will succeed only to the extent that I continually recognize and embrace my incompetence. I will not attain my desire if I do not love my failures.

If you sincerely love your incompetence, you cannot fail to succeed.

^^

Because spiritual poverty is so devastating, its ability to deliver is so profound.

^^

Let's say you loved chocolate donuts; let's say you were crazy about them. And then you found a secret way to nearly continuously obtain and enjoy eating them. For having found this secret, you probably would not think of yourself more noble and wise than others. Nor does the apophatic mystic consider himself more noble or wise for having found his treasure. He found his treasure hidden within spiritual poverty, and he does not want to lose it by having pretensions.

^^

If you are afraid of losing deliverance, you most certainly will lose it. If you fully appreciate that there is nothing you can do to securely keep it, you will probably not lose it. In this strange endeavor, loosening up is better than tightening; carelessness is more effective than carefulness.

^^

While many other paths don't ring true for me, at least not at first glance, what rings the most untrue for me is the thought that I can be certain any of these other paths are untrue, or that I can be sure my own is true. My way feels compelling to me at this moment, and it seems that I can retain that compelling quality only to the degree that I avoid making gratuitous comparative claims.

^^

I am too selfishly interested in avoiding what harms my aims, to criticize what I perceive to be your mistakes. Furthermore, I am not really sure that you are mistaken.

^^

I can offer you intimacy for the moment. And I am not sure that we will ever have more time than this.

^^

I best embrace all my abilities and all of my deficits. I even need to embrace and own my ego's pathetic attempts to outfox yours.

^^

The sage gets angry

If the ego-perspective has not been sufficiently subordinated to the unitary perspective, the person who has made significant progress in mystical cultivation may still become upset whenever he is reminded of his remaining deficits. If the ego-perspective has been subordinated, these deficits are not a problem; they can be employed to generate alchemical transformation. Both "good" and "bad" emotional reactions provide transmutable energy, and so each of them is equally useful in the work of internal alchemy. Once we learn how to apply it, there is no need to get angry about being angered.

^^

Nietzsche's eternal return

You don't have to disprove Nietzsche's pessimistic proposal of the "eternal return," or dismiss Ecclesiastes' "there is no new thing under the sun." You can have fun here in this world for no known reason at all. Through grace you can realize there is no need to justify your love for life and your embrace of the totality which life bestows.

The unreasonable ability to love unconditionally is found through mystical deliverance. It is a joy to be freed to say "yes" to life without apology.

∧∧∧∧∧∧∧∧∧∧∧∧∧∧∧∧∧∧∧∧∧∧∧∧∧∧∧∧∧∧∧∧∧∧∧∧∧

"Look over there. Notice how shockingly uninteresting those people are. If you ever attain deliverance from yourself, you will then be astonished to see the richly intricate designs with which each of them has been wrought. You will be able to notice that every one of them has become almost as exquisitely fascinating to you as yourself."

Rawley Creed

∧∧∧∧∧∧∧∧∧∧∧∧∧∧∧∧∧∧∧∧∧∧∧∧∧∧∧∧∧∧∧∧∧∧∧∧∧

I don't indulge in blame or guilt. My guess is that every creature is doing the best it can with the capabilities it has.

∧∧∧∧∧∧∧∧∧∧∧∧∧∧∧∧∧∧∧∧∧∧∧∧∧∧∧∧∧∧∧∧∧∧∧∧∧

I usually *love* everyone. When I don't, it is because something about myself is annoying me. When it occurs, my hatred is self-hatred. At those times you, the other person, remind me too much of myself.

By *love* I mean having a sense that all others have the same precious value as myself. It does not mean I won't kill you if you are trying to kill me or my family. When Jesus said "Love your enemies," it is interesting that he seems to have recognized that there really are enemies you may have to defend yourself against. But it is superfluous to hate them.

Interestingly, sometimes if your enemies sense your love for them, they stop being your enemies. That one is a little hard for some of my sister and brother countrymen to wrap their minds around.

^^

"I was picking lettuce and I heard a voice saying, 'Want too much from me and I will take everything you have away; ask for a little and I will give you more than you would guess possible.'"

Carla Ansantina

^^

I don't know whether or not it is true, but I tell my ego there are no avatars. That way it does not waste my time trying to be one.

^^

Depression is painful, and mania ends up causing even more painful depression. Tempered mania is quite nice.

^^

Don't be too quick to criticize other folks' religion. A certain amount of self-deception may be requisite to sanity. It may be a question of finding the right dose of credulity.

^^

Within wisdom traditions, the most universally condemned heresy is not taking dedication to the spiritual path seriously. In applying the apophatic tool, neither preemptive gravity nor preemptive capriciousness is warranted. The apophaticist has not yet decided if it is the fool or the wise person who is the more prudent.

^^

"The problem is that God left a fair number of loose ends. Whenever I feel like making myself miserable, I try to make sense of them."

Carla Ansantina

^^

A difficult mystical skill is making Great Doubt and Great Annoyance into your great friends.

^^

Rapture is delightful. But a mystic learns how to enjoy any ordinary moment so well that he does not care if he ever again experiences rapture.

^^

清 Qing: Clarity

The mystic has obtained a clear, comprehensive look at herself. And so she won't be horrified by anything you say, or anything you have done.

∧∧∧∧∧∧∧∧∧∧∧∧∧∧∧∧∧∧∧∧∧∧∧∧∧∧∧∧∧∧∧∧∧∧∧∧∧∧

There is usually no information that can threaten a pragmatic apophaticist, because he generally has no hold on anything, and so he has nothing to lose. But whenever he does try to grab hold of something which is nothing, he becomes the most frightened person of all.

∧∧∧∧∧∧∧∧∧∧∧∧∧∧∧∧∧∧∧∧∧∧∧∧∧∧∧∧∧∧∧∧∧∧∧∧∧∧

I'm afraid I am too much of an elitist to criticize the religions of the masses. Morbidly narcissistic, I am much more interested in and nauseated by my own flaws.

∧∧∧∧∧∧∧∧∧∧∧∧∧∧∧∧∧∧∧∧∧∧∧∧∧∧∧∧∧∧∧∧∧∧∧∧∧∧

I don't blame or make excuses for any Gods. If there are any, they understand why I don't. If there are none, they also understand.

∧∧∧∧∧∧∧∧∧∧∧∧∧∧∧∧∧∧∧∧∧∧∧∧∧∧∧∧∧∧∧∧∧∧∧∧∧∧

If you want Resilience, you need to include taking her sister Ambiguity with you. You will learn to be tenacious without needing to have a reason.

∧∧∧∧∧∧∧∧∧∧∧∧∧∧∧∧∧∧∧∧∧∧∧∧∧∧∧∧∧∧∧∧∧∧∧∧∧∧

It has taken me a long time to find out that the most transformative meditation is often available when I don't feel like meditation, or when I don't have enough time to meditate, or when my mind is most neurotically vexed, my emotions most unstable, my fear extreme, or all of the above happening at once. Finding a small place of stillness amid that turmoil, even for a few brief minutes, will increase my mystical aptitude more than an hour of blissfully serene meditation.

∧∧

I don't feel any *obligation* to love you. I would not feel guilty if I hated you. I don't actually have a reason why it is that I am so fond of you and everyone else, no matter what you do. I don't mind if you hate me; I will love you no less if you do.

∧∧

That tendency which causes you to be proud of your tribe or nation is perfectly natural and legitimate. The Germans call it *Wesenswille*, the natural compulsion to assert the value of your essence and that of your tribe. But to assert or deny such values are notions which the mystic wants to be free of.

∧∧

"Its uselessness is what makes it so useful."
Zhuangzi, chapter 26

Apophaticism, if embraced as a comprehensive ideology, will fail. If examined carefully, it can be shown to have fatal logical flaws. And it is this failure to be foolproof which makes it so useful as a tool. By failing as a truth, it becomes successful as a tool.

Its poverty of truth allows for an ignorance which transports you to the mystical threshold, but at the threshold it fails to show you what you need to do to get across. It is that final failure that allows grace to take you across.

∧∧

What can help you attain spiritual poverty

A major contributor to spiritual poverty is the candid recognition by the apophaticist that a believer might turn out to be much wiser than he. For all the apophaticist knows, the believer* who believes in a final transcendent deliverance may be factually correct. Furthermore the believer may have an ultimately stronger and more enduring sense of well-being.

The apophaticist does have a convincing sense of what he himself needs to do and not to do. But he has no sense of what another person might need to do. And he has no sense of which of the multitude of wisdom paths is comparatively the wisest. His path might turn out to be the shortest on wisdom.

*(The same holds for the denier; she might turn out to be wiser than the apophaticist.)

∧∧

Blessed is the artless fool who innocently pleads with his God to help him believe that God exists.

∧∧

The only evidence found that is objective is evidence which is subjectively experienced. That subjective evidence is the experienced fact that something exists, and that something is also a subject who is aware of its existence. All I can know for sure is that something is happening. Not being able to expand the certainty of any knowledge beyond this small amount of truth might help me maintain spiritual poverty.

∧∧∧∧∧∧∧∧∧∧∧∧∧∧∧∧∧∧∧∧∧∧∧∧∧∧∧∧∧∧∧∧∧∧∧∧

The total relief of existential tension might be a futile pursuit. Instead of that aim, the apophatic mystic attempts to obtain and maintain a serene space within the tension.

∧∧∧∧∧∧∧∧∧∧∧∧∧∧∧∧∧∧∧∧∧∧∧∧∧∧∧∧∧∧∧∧∧∧∧∧

To experience ecstasy, to get outside of your normal self, you have to ruthlessly and objectively examine your behavior. And paradoxically you also must remember that you are already perfectly fine the way you are. Your goal as an apophaticist is a better performance and not the realization of sainthood. From the apophatic point of view, sainthood appears to be a mistaken goal, a futile pursuit. As Carla Ansantina says, "You can only be as good as God allows you to be."

∧∧∧∧∧∧∧∧∧∧∧∧∧∧∧∧∧∧∧∧∧∧∧∧∧∧∧∧∧∧∧∧∧∧∧∧

Are you feeling unsettled today? Tell yourself that this is a normal condition and then find the island of equanimity within this turbulent sea.

∧∧∧∧∧∧∧∧∧∧∧∧∧∧∧∧∧∧∧∧∧∧∧∧∧∧∧∧∧∧∧∧∧∧∧∧

"Rushing is okay, but rushing without presence is a waste of God's time."

Carla Ansantina

∧∧∧∧∧∧∧∧∧∧∧∧∧∧∧∧∧∧∧∧∧∧∧∧∧∧∧∧∧∧∧∧∧∧∧∧∧

Despite my most vigilant efforts, my ego is constantly building the illusion of a stable world within which to ensconce itself. It takes nearly a God to force it to surrender its work so that I can become free to simply enjoy the mysterious wonder of being here with all of you.

∧∧∧∧∧∧∧∧∧∧∧∧∧∧∧∧∧∧∧∧∧∧∧∧∧∧∧∧∧∧∧∧∧∧∧∧∧

The interesting thing is that the ability to know that "I am always already okay" is an ability that seems to be just as rare among "successful" people as it is among beggars. Hardly anyone has recognized the archetypal meaning in Luther's "faith not works."

There is nothing to do except learn how and why to realize there is nothing to do.

∧∧∧∧∧∧∧∧∧∧∧∧∧∧∧∧∧∧∧∧∧∧∧∧∧∧∧∧∧∧∧∧∧∧∧∧∧

Needlessness

Find your dinner and a roof over your head, keeping it dry from the rain. These are your practical needs. Also keep one of your inner eyes on the recognition of *needlessness*. Needlessness is the place where love alone is entirely sufficient. Love is the domain where all of your practical needs, as well as your needs for religions and atheisms, have vanished. Love is needless. Love needs no more than itself.

∧∧∧∧∧∧∧∧∧∧∧∧∧∧∧∧∧∧∧∧∧∧∧∧∧∧∧∧∧∧∧∧∧∧∧∧∧

Bataille and Luther

It is fascinating to read of the genius of Georges Bataille as he floundered about the irredeemable ambiguity of his world. It is splendid to be able to look back, to not have come of age in the '20s, '30s, '40s, or '50s when the human mind still believed it was capable of fixing the world; when it still believed that there are political, sociological, and religious formulations which can solve the fundamental problems. From our later perspective, we can see the futility of these dreams and now we can truly appreciate Luther's "faith not works," and Bataille's railings against "project." We now live in a completely unsettled but blessed time. Bataille and Luther have helped set us free to fully enjoy ourselves, to love without reason.

^^^

I think there is a place within consciousness to create one's own gods, and one's own spiritual path. While Sartre might call this "bad faith," his own creation of a non-deist spirituality is also not warranted by any objective evidence.

^^^

The fact is that we don't need any objective evidence to validate mysticism. Subjective evidence shows us we can be creatively happy for no objective reason.

^^^

When I hold on too tightly, it is a futile attempt to violate the dynamic unity of opposites.

^^^

The ego wants more than mystical ability. It wants recognition and privilege. These desires put a low ceiling on mystical potential.

∧∧∧

Even if it is small, watch it carefully. You don't want your fame to outrun and thereby diminish your ability.

∧∧∧

Have you ever had a *Kali* experience? I don't know what, if any, factual basis there is to the experience, but I find the fruit of the vision illuminating and useful. A number of times I have experienced this archetypal Mother who bears and later kills her children. In the immediacy of the moment in which I was fully present to her, she stood ready to give her unlimited love to me. It was not a conditional love; like a true mother she held nothing back regardless of my equivocation, despite my fascination with her and yet horror at her being. What was perhaps most strange to me is that she encouraged me to express a compassionate under-standing toward those who unequivocally hate her. She allowed me to realize that their abhorrence was reasoned and natural.

I have learned to love this primordial Mother nearly as completely and candidly as she loves me. The startling ecstatic transport which I experience each time at the moment of our encounter causes me to lose interest in the expected final outcome of our relation-ship.

∧∧∧

As a religion evolves, it often includes a systematic attempt to civilize the sacred, to tame out the demonic elements of the mystery. Mature religion tends to restrain the terrorizing and glorious potentials found at the core of the sacred—potentials generated by the unbridled volatility released at the climatic point where opposites are unified. Conventional religion, not mysticism, is probably the prudent choice for most people, allowing as it does a healthy distance from the sacred.

∧∧∧∧∧∧∧∧∧∧∧∧∧∧∧∧∧∧∧∧∧∧∧∧∧∧∧∧∧∧∧∧∧∧∧∧∧∧

In pursuit of mystical ecstasy, you have had to open yourself up to an array of unpredictable external and internal forces. These unreigned powers injure your psychic stability decreasing your functional competence. You are noticeably handicapped at many of the practical tasks of everyday life. But your handicap allows you to better recognize and more effectively deal with another larger handicap, one that universally causes anxiety among human beings: the inability to master the terms of one's own existence. By being able to notice this innate flaw in everyone, you are able to intimately and promptly engage each and every person who you encounter. The other person usually will not consciously understand how you are able to so effortlessly achieve this communion with them, nor are they aware of the price you have paid to attain this ability.

∧∧∧∧∧∧∧∧∧∧∧∧∧∧∧∧∧∧∧∧∧∧∧∧∧∧∧∧∧∧∧∧∧∧∧∧∧∧

Be predictable enough for other people to feel comfortable near you. Be unpredictable enough so that you can love and enjoy each one of them.

∧∧∧∧∧∧∧∧∧∧∧∧∧∧∧∧∧∧∧∧∧∧∧∧∧∧∧∧∧∧∧∧∧∧∧∧∧∧

"Theology is an affront to God."

Rawley Creed

∧∧∧∧∧∧∧∧∧∧∧∧∧∧∧∧∧∧∧∧∧∧∧∧∧∧∧∧∧∧∧∧∧∧∧∧∧∧∧

The thin membrane of sanity

Keep enough insanity out so that you don't lose your mind. Let enough in so that you can enjoy yourself.

∧∧∧∧∧∧∧∧∧∧∧∧∧∧∧∧∧∧∧∧∧∧∧∧∧∧∧∧∧∧∧∧∧∧∧∧∧∧∧

The deeper mind is focused on the immediate, all of its ends and means arise from the moment. I am ignorant of what these ends and means are until the moment they arise. This ignorance is the "pobreza espiritual" (spiritual poverty) which St. John of the Cross was fond of.

∧∧∧∧∧∧∧∧∧∧∧∧∧∧∧∧∧∧∧∧∧∧∧∧∧∧∧∧∧∧∧∧∧∧∧∧∧∧∧

"Reality is whatever shows up right here."

Rawley Creed

∧∧∧∧∧∧∧∧∧∧∧∧∧∧∧∧∧∧∧∧∧∧∧∧∧∧∧∧∧∧∧∧∧∧∧∧∧∧∧

In the apophatic approach, death is not defeated, nor is the thought of it banished. It simply becomes another tool to use in the technology of ecstasy. A powerful prospect, the thought of death can effectively concentrate attention in the immediacy of each moment. There, death's power is subverted and used to generate the enjoyment of life. This strange phenomenon is possible because for the mystic the essence of death is nearly always *not yet*.

∧∧∧∧∧∧∧∧∧∧∧∧∧∧∧∧∧∧∧∧∧∧∧∧∧∧∧∧∧∧∧∧∧∧∧∧∧∧∧

I may not cleanse my heart of stuff that most people think needs to be cleaned out. And my motive may be unseemly. I cleanse my heart for the pure pleasure of it.

∧∧∧∧∧∧∧∧∧∧∧∧∧∧∧∧∧∧∧∧∧∧∧∧∧∧∧∧∧∧∧∧∧∧∧∧∧

One day I said to myself, "Let's forget about ever finishing the book. Let me just appropriate the pain of this dreadful writing process and apply it to cultivate mystical growth." After that I was much happier about doing the writing.

∧∧∧∧∧∧∧∧∧∧∧∧∧∧∧∧∧∧∧∧∧∧∧∧∧∧∧∧∧∧∧∧∧∧∧∧∧

When I sense how little substance I might turn out to have, I sometimes tumult downward and crash through the floor of hell. At other times, that same sense frees me from the usual weight of my ego, and I shoot up beyond the limits of the imaginable.

∧∧∧∧∧∧∧∧∧∧∧∧∧∧∧∧∧∧∧∧∧∧∧∧∧∧∧∧∧∧∧∧∧∧∧∧∧

The transgressions of mystical love

Mystical love (love without reason) is often found in direct opposition to moral sensitivity. We often forget the historical context when we read the story of Jesus halting an entirely legal execution of an adulterous woman. His love flagrantly transgressed the ethical sensitivities of his time.

Transgression is a tricky area to navigate. At times transgressing the social conventions allows one to delve more deeply into mystical love. At other times forbidden behavior drastically injures love. There are transgressions which deliver you to heaven, while others send you to hell.

∧∧

"Keep most of your transgressions to yourself. Published to the world, most of them will do no one any good."

Rawley Creed

∧∧

The adept fairly quickly learns how mystically effective excess and transgression as forms of mystical cultivation can be. It is usually more difficult to realize how powerfully transformative moderation can be. There is "a time for all seasons."

∧∧

Transgression for mystical cultivation

Many acts of transgression are like shots of narcotics, only good for a few moments and then soon unnecessarily causing distance between you and another person. It may be unfair to judge the mystical value of Georges Bataille's writing by looking at the tragic phase near the end of his life. But it may give us some evidence of the futility of glorifying the forbidden as a means of mystical transcendence, of making such practices into one's only God. (Friedrich Nietzsche's dreadful end may be another example of the potential effects of some perspectives on transgression.) Transgression is annoyingly like a number of other things; one needs to be prudent when choosing what to violate. If not prudent, instead of transcendence, one might merely end up with degeneration and a decline in mystical ability.

∧∧

Sometimes I tacitly assume another person has a childish, bizarre, degenerate, or mistaken appreciation of existence and its purpose. To thusly objectify another is a failure to appreciate the status of the person as an autonomous subject. I objectify the other person when I rightly or wrongly estimate that his experience of his world is less valid than my own. When I do this, I lose the ability to obtain what I actually want the most—not a validation of my purported truth but an intimate connection. Through an intimate connection, we will both find what we need.

∧∧∧∧∧∧∧∧∧∧∧∧∧∧∧∧∧∧∧∧∧∧∧∧∧∧∧∧∧∧∧∧∧∧∧∧∧∧

Ernest Becker said that because of our existential condition we are innately manic-depressive. To moderate mood swings and, more importantly, to maximize the intensity of deliverance, it is good to have a simultaneous sense of yourself as both an angel and a cockroach. Each of those beings has sacred and practical value.

∧∧∧∧∧∧∧∧∧∧∧∧∧∧∧∧∧∧∧∧∧∧∧∧∧∧∧∧∧∧∧∧∧∧∧∧∧∧

The most important desire to conquer is the desire for spiritual mastery. Love your inescapable mediocrity and you will do extremely well.

∧∧∧∧∧∧∧∧∧∧∧∧∧∧∧∧∧∧∧∧∧∧∧∧∧∧∧∧∧∧∧∧∧∧∧∧∧∧

Blessed are the Gods who fail you

Whatever your God is—deism, atheism, material-ism, agnosticism, poly-theism, apophaticism, etc.—if you are unconditionally faithful, recklessly devoted to it, your God will almost certainly fail you sooner or later. On that day, your disappointment will be immense; it may knock you down and put you into a dreadful despair. But if you survive such a fall, you will be in a good position to find out a rarely told secret. With luck you will have just enough vitality left to gaze around hell's floor. It is there, where you have nothing more to lose, that you may stumble upon the mystic's mystery: *nothing*, by itself, can surprisingly generate everything you need for satisfaction. Whatever caused your existence has put this strange capacity within your being. In hell you can find it most effectively—an enduring sense of well-being and all-embracing love—with no reasonable explanation. Your reckless open-hearted devotion to your God, or to your denial of a God, has paid off nicely. Amazing grace.

∧∧∧∧∧∧∧∧∧∧∧∧∧∧∧∧∧∧∧∧∧∧∧∧∧∧∧∧∧∧∧∧∧∧∧∧∧

"If the fool would persist in his folly, he would become wise."

William Blake

∧∧∧∧∧∧∧∧∧∧∧∧∧∧∧∧∧∧∧∧∧∧∧∧∧∧∧∧∧∧∧∧∧∧∧∧∧

"This nothingness is her falling into the certainty of knowing nothing and wanting nothing. And this nothingness of which we speak, called Love, gives her all."

Margaret Porete
(translated by Thomas Hall)

∧∧∧∧∧∧∧∧∧∧∧∧∧∧∧∧∧∧∧∧∧∧∧∧∧∧∧∧∧∧∧∧∧∧∧∧∧

Effective forgiveness runs deep and is all-inclusive. The mystic not only forgives the other person as best she can; just as importantly she forgives herself for any degree of failure to forgive.

∧∧∧∧∧∧∧∧∧∧∧∧∧∧∧∧∧∧∧∧∧∧∧∧∧∧∧∧∧∧∧∧∧∧∧∧∧∧

"I heard God say she does not expect me to act any better but would not mind if I learned how to be happier."

Carla Ansantina

∧∧∧∧∧∧∧∧∧∧∧∧∧∧∧∧∧∧∧∧∧∧∧∧∧∧∧∧∧∧∧∧∧∧∧∧∧∧

"This guy called Crazy Uncle used to hang around the depot. He never said much, but one day he pulled me aside and explained everything to me. Uncle showed me how everything in this world is perfect, and why that includes everything that is not."

Rawley Creed

∧∧∧∧∧∧∧∧∧∧∧∧∧∧∧∧∧∧∧∧∧∧∧∧∧∧∧∧∧∧∧∧∧∧∧∧∧∧

One of the most interesting questions is how our characterization of "whatever-it-is" affects our ability to love.

∧∧∧∧∧∧∧∧∧∧∧∧∧∧∧∧∧∧∧∧∧∧∧∧∧∧∧∧∧∧∧∧∧∧∧∧∧∧

There are ways to heal from a catastrophic loss without reducing the gravity of the loss by convincing yourself that there is a metaphysical justification for what has happened.

∧∧∧∧∧∧∧∧∧∧∧∧∧∧∧∧∧∧∧∧∧∧∧∧∧∧∧∧∧∧∧∧∧∧∧∧∧∧

When meditating, you are free to enjoy bliss or alternatively wrestle with your demons. When a certain level of ability is reached, either one of these is as satisfying as the other.

∧∧∧∧∧∧∧∧∧∧∧∧∧∧∧∧∧∧∧∧∧∧∧∧∧∧∧∧∧∧∧∧∧∧∧∧∧∧

Hatred is evidence of self-deception.

^^^

Wherever your ego is weakest your psychic forces are defensively embattled, consciously or subconsciously. Winning these battles is a matter of realizing that you can easily afford to lose them.

^^^

In every spiritual tradition we find the theme of *liberation*. It is variously called deliverance, moksha, release, etc. What is unique in the spirituality of Zhuangzi is that he has identified a type of *liberation* which requires no metaphysical basis. He emphasizes that there is no known rational basis for his release from angst.

^^^

I don't think the myth of "a fall" rings true. My sense is that whatever force created this, she put it together exactly how she wanted it to work. I don't like the way it sometimes works, but I don't know how it could have been put together any better.

^^^

If you have realized the know-how that lets you transform negative emotional states into the fuel of transformation, you have 95% of what you need to obtain mental ecstasy. 15 seconds of alchemically bathing in vexation is worth 15 minutes of meditation.

^^^

If you can't see any goodness in your enemy, you have also missed seeing a huge portion of your own.

∧∧

The peace-maker is best to have a sense of both morality and amorality. Believing that one's opponent is fundamentally "evil" is not that useful.

∧∧

The so-called "absence of God" potentially provides one of the most forceful manifestations of mystical presence. Here is the formula for this ecstasy: Enjoy, but don't take any unusual occurrence too seriously. Find that place within the psyche that graciously responds to the commonplace. Learn how to center yourself in this serene disposition as continually as you can. Through this disposition you can find the most enduring intensity of unconditional love, the jewel of deliverance.

∧∧

"God is the only one responsible for evil, and she loves us no less for pointing it out. She gently lets us know that we are wasting our time when we judge which among us non-gods are good, and which are evil."

Carla Ansantina

∧∧

For those who worry about taking on another person's negativity or illness:

To the degree that I have nothing to lose within me, except this moment of love, nothing but love in the other person can attach itself to me. Learning the "how-to" of emptying out all the other stuff is a long, difficult, but wonderful task.

∧∧∧∧∧∧∧∧∧∧∧∧∧∧∧∧∧∧∧∧∧∧∧∧∧∧∧∧∧∧∧∧∧∧∧∧∧∧

"Embody the dao"
Zhuangzi, chapter 22

The mystical disposition is felt in the body, sometimes it is a "taste," sometimes it is described as a "glow." It is a visceral sense which changes the world of the mystic in a manner quite different than the context provided by the mind. The body knows something which the mind cannot grasp. Zhuangzi said that his mouth was unable to make words for it.

∧∧∧∧∧∧∧∧∧∧∧∧∧∧∧∧∧∧∧∧∧∧∧∧∧∧∧∧∧∧∧∧∧∧∧∧∧∧

"We humans are fundamentally stupid; it is not our fault, but being stupid is no problem for the enlightened. For them it is not a handicap."

Rawley Creed

∧∧∧∧∧∧∧∧∧∧∧∧∧∧∧∧∧∧∧∧∧∧∧∧∧∧∧∧∧∧∧∧∧∧∧∧∧∧

Volatility in meditation

Rage, agitation, dysphoria, yelling, a sense of failure, a sense of ennui—all of these kinds of emotional turmoil generate power. This power can be transmuted and its energy harnessed to run a process that shatters many of the structures the ego has built. These can be rebuilt in a manner which will then allow a nearly invulnerable sense of well-being, the serenity of "knowing nothing."

Eros and ethics

Ludwig Wittgenstein said, "Ethics and aesthetics are one and the same." From an apophatic view, the pleasure principle is the only coherent explanation for what is called "ethical behavior." What I like I call "good," and what I don't like I call "bad." I do things which bring *me* pleasure and avoid things that cause *me* pain. Often what causes you pain will also cause me pain, but often it will not.

To be coherent and transparent, an understanding of ethics needs to appreciate how what are called "ethical decisions" are decisions which are fundamentally based on the pleasure principle.

Any attempt to avoid this subjectivity and try to claim a universal ethics will invariably end up in self-deceit. As Jesus said, "You see the dirt in your neighbor's eye but don't see the plank in your own." When this is fully understood, one no longer finds any reason to disdain another being. Free of that rancor, life becomes an exquisite pleasure; here, an optimal level of eros has been reached.

∧∧∧∧∧∧∧∧∧∧∧∧∧∧∧∧∧∧∧∧∧∧∧∧∧∧∧∧∧∧∧∧∧∧∧∧∧

Eros and St. John of the Cross

St. John of the Cross wisely advises giving up the desire for spiritual sweetness (golosina) and gluttony (gula). But he is carefully neglecting to mention that by forgoing these pleasures he is aiming at an even more intense pleasure. By characterizing this pleasure as "God," he is presenting it as something we *should do,* and not something we would *want to enjoy*. Wanting to enjoy something is a bit too unseemly for this saint.

The important thing here, on a practical level, is that it is useful to avoid striving for rapture and other dramatic spiritual experiences, and instead go for a larger and more widely found pleasure, an ecstasy which provides the ideal combination of intensity and endurance. That is the ecstasy one can discover in St. John's "dark night of the soul" experience, and there learn how to have it available both day and night. On the other hand, spontaneous rapture is not a problem; it is a blessing.

∧∧∧∧∧∧∧∧∧∧∧∧∧∧∧∧∧∧∧∧∧∧∧∧∧∧∧∧∧∧∧∧∧∧∧∧

A generous understanding

When someone tells me they are having a "direct experience of God," I experientially understand what they are saying, even if I might not share their theological conclusions.

∧∧∧∧∧∧∧∧∧∧∧∧∧∧∧∧∧∧∧∧∧∧∧∧∧∧∧∧∧∧∧∧∧∧∧∧

I question Georges Bataille's fondness for transgressive behavior. To attain the mystical experience—ecstasy—one does not have to violate the social conventions; instead, one needs to violate the conventions of one's own mind. One needs to get far beyond the methods the mind employs to find happiness. When Bataille endorses the systematic application of transgressive behavior, he is violating his own condemnation of "project." He is contriving an experience, and not surrendering to the liberating dynamics of what he called "inner experience."

∧∧∧∧∧∧∧∧∧∧∧∧∧∧∧∧∧∧∧∧∧∧∧∧∧∧∧∧∧∧∧∧∧∧∧∧∧

Georges Bataille had an agnostic, if not atheistic, approach to mystical experience. He found that holding the idea of a God would circumscribe what is a sovereign and apparently illimitable experience.

∧∧∧∧∧∧∧∧∧∧∧∧∧∧∧∧∧∧∧∧∧∧∧∧∧∧∧∧∧∧∧∧∧∧∧∧∧

Martin Luther's "faith not works" and Georges Bataille's condemnation of "project" are analogues. It is not important what I do, or what I avoid doing. The key to deliverance is my present psycho-physical disposition.

∧∧∧∧∧∧∧∧∧∧∧∧∧∧∧∧∧∧∧∧∧∧∧∧∧∧∧∧∧∧∧∧∧∧∧∧∧

Mystical ecstasy is an art where the ill effects of an event can be transcended by going more deeply into the experience. At the center nothing is amiss.

∧∧∧∧∧∧∧∧∧∧∧∧∧∧∧∧∧∧∧∧∧∧∧∧∧∧∧∧∧∧∧∧∧∧∧∧∧

Rage

The world of the pragmatic apophaticist is not "all right." But whatever is not right is serviceable, if one knows how to use it. Because all of it is serviceable for this mystic, it is the source of a nearly unshakable sense of well-being. What is difficult to understand is that the mystic's rage against the way some things are—for example rage that there are those who suffer terribly because they have not learned how to mystically utilize everything—is a rage which can also be quite serviceable and appropriate.

∧∧∧∧∧∧∧∧∧∧∧∧∧∧∧∧∧∧∧∧∧∧∧∧∧∧∧∧∧∧∧∧∧∧∧∧∧

Apophatic mysticism is an agnostic mysticism, but unlike the approach of typical agnosticism, there is no waiting until something is proven. This mysticism proceeds without proving anything; it entails a surrender to an experience which is beyond the capacity of the human mind's ability to authenticate. The apophatic mystic participates in the experience simply because it is so compelling, not because its validity has been analytically demonstrated.

^^^

When one is suffering, if one has an open-heart, that is to say if one is open to any possibility—no matter how unimaginable—one will do okay. One is safe as long as one remains curious.

And if you want to try the apophatic approach, forget about the prescription which we hear so often: "Never lose faith." The thought of faith does no good when one is in the deepest suffering, the "dark night of the soul." That is because loss of faith is the defining aspect of this brutal condition; lost faith is the very reason one is suffering so miserably. So don't bother worrying yourself about losing faith at this point. But on the other hand, don't lose your curiosity; that can be fatal.

The aim of pragmatic apophatic mysticism is to optimize happiness. This is done through employing a number of methods and these include accepting, reflecting on, and absorbing an appropriate amount of unhappiness. Unhappiness has no intrinsic value; no prizes or special status accrue to the unhappy. But unhappiness has a curious ability to be adeptly employed as a doorway to the realm of non-contingent happiness. It can be the best friend one ever finds.

The folly of trying to be more lovable

This book treats a certain mystical methodology. By applying this methodology the practitioner will be able to more deeply engage and enjoy the presence of the unspeakable. The problem with such books as this is that there is almost always an implicit assertion that a human being lacks a degree of value if he chooses not to put a method such as this into practice. There is usually an unspoken assumption that a "good" person needs to apply this or another methodology. Most of the world's wisdom literature tells us that we all should be doing something "worthwhile." To do nothing to improve oneself is taken to be failure. I suspect that this commonly accepted demand has questionable validity. Let us apply our methodologies, but let us not fool ourselves about any need to increase or even maintain our value. My strong sense is that there is something in the ground of our being, a whatever-it-is, which loves us and holds us to be immutably lovable for no reason at all.

Even if the daughter or son is eternally prodigal, they are loved no less. The love of the unspeakable is never withdrawn.

Love does not compel a performance or a success, demands no allegiance, no recognition, is not jealous, does not punish, is endlessly indulgent, demands no goodness. Love defends no idea, insists on nothing, wants for nothing. It makes no claims, denies no assertions, needs no believing, does not forbid doubt, is not proud. Love blames no one, despises no one, finds value in everyone and everything. It requires no rationale, no proof, no external validation. Love claims no privilege, calculates no debts, tallies no obligations, does not deem itself to be right or wrong, does not insist on gravity. Love is sufficient unto itself. Love says, "Come closer to me if you will, and you will soon find out what I am about."

I will only be completely free to realize and share unconditional love if and when I realize that love never asks anything of me. By applying effective methods I may get better at realizing how much I am loved. But whatever I do or fail to do, I will never be loved any more or any less. The paradox is that if I think that I can ever become more worthy of love, I will be less able to realize how extraordinarily I am loved and always will be.

∧∧

Across the spectrum of various spiritual and religious traditions there seems to be a number of similar patterns observed; we find similarities in the literature which might be called generic archetypal realizations. There seems to be what Carl Jung called a collective unconsciousness, a universally shared collection of spiritual dynamics. The generic spiritual realization takes different forms in the different traditions, and we might to our advantage reflect on the question of which forms are more or less effective in serving the aims put forward by individual seekers.

∧∧

Purgative suffering in a nutshell

How exquisitely painful and joyful is the suffering that is undergone when we clean out everything that we thought we could be certain of—philosophical, religious, practical, and pragmatic—with the result that all of it except love becomes absent of any fundamental meaning. Love remains intact simply because it apparently needs no "why." When I am in the zone of "no why," my sense of ecstasy is able to incorporate suffering in a manner so that even suffering brings forth joy. In that zone, I find myself in love with everything.

^^

To fully enjoy life, one is best to come to terms with death. This coming to terms may include raging against the fact of death. In the wake of that rage one can often find a mystical opening that leads to deliverance.

^^

Sincerity is passion with openness.

^^

The problem with a perfection-focused model of spirituality is that if there is a potential perfection to be had, it is obviously something one would seek and need to find sooner or later. By seeking this perfection, one is attempting to achieve invulnerability, one of the hallmarks of perfection. The problem for the apophaticist is that her aim is love; the root of this love is imperfection, a vulnerability which is only found with spiritual poverty.

^^

The key is *nothing*

Generally speaking, being encouraged to think positive is good advice. And so why is the mystic equally interested in negativity? The more you accomplish, the more you are likely to forget to realize that you have nothing guaranteed. However, that *nothing* is the key to deliverance. This is why the mystics express the desire to be "ruined." They want to be rid of everything that is weighing them down, everything that is keeping them from ecstasy. They want the destruction of whatever "success" is preventing their liberation.

∧∧∧∧∧∧∧∧∧∧∧∧∧∧∧∧∧∧∧∧∧∧∧∧∧∧∧∧∧∧∧∧∧∧∧∧∧∧∧

"To hold one's way as the best for all is to ignore the uniqueness of each person's ways. Tailors may know this better than some mystics."

Ruling Barragan-Yanez

Rare is the mystic who does not claim his way to be the best way for everyone. Zhuangzi was one of those rare ones.

∧∧∧∧∧∧∧∧∧∧∧∧∧∧∧∧∧∧∧∧∧∧∧∧∧∧∧∧∧∧∧∧∧∧∧∧∧∧∧

The mystic nearly reaches her aim and realizes why this nearness is called "failure." But at this point she knows that even failure has to be surrendered in order to successfully cross the final threshold.

∧∧∧∧∧∧∧∧∧∧∧∧∧∧∧∧∧∧∧∧∧∧∧∧∧∧∧∧∧∧∧∧∧∧∧∧∧∧∧

Folly

There is an implicit *a priori* which is found in almost all religion and mysticism. That *a priori* asserts that life *must* be taken seriously. On a practical level this attitude is useful for personal health and safety. But on a spiritual level it is an unhelpful arrogance.

Folly is the muse who remedies this arrogance. She helps us find a spirituality free of pretensions.

^^^

The dangers of writing about mysticism

To write a book one has to know how to succeed. To realize a practice of mysticism one has to learn how to fail.

^^^

No final remedy

To realize that there might be no final remedy for the human situation, and to accept that disturbing lack of guarantee graciously—that seems to be the way toward attaining the optimal freedom to enjoy life. That is the path toward realizing a love and happiness which is unreasonable and unconditional. Not anchored by one's sense of reason, one becomes potentially able to grasp the untellable secret of grace. Through that grace, the potential for ecstasy becomes unlimited, the sense of well-being nearly undauntable.

^^^

From experience, I can report that the mystical experience—the experience of the presence of the whatever-it-is—is so compelling that the question of "verifying the true nature of what is happening" becomes a moot point for me. The thought of the possibility that the experience "is a delusion" is of no consequence. Whatever the experience is, the exquisite pleasure of it leaves me with no doubt that I will continue to proceed in a manner that allows its recurrence as often and as intensely as possible.

At times we despair of not being able to find any certainty that anything is of ultimate consequence. The astonishing beauty of love is that it requires no certainty.

^^^

At the heart of the apophatic method is the surrender of agenda. The motive is to enjoy an extreme pleasure—love—to enjoy life by intimately communicating with every other being.

^^^

This is hard: I need to continually remember that whatever I am feeling—good, bad, beautiful, ugly—what I am feeling right now is precisely the manifestation of the presence of the unspeakable, what some call "the divine presence."

^^^

Is spirituality simply a stunning example of the placebo effect?

In recent years there is increased medical research focused on the so-called placebo effect. There been numerous examples of subjects in experiments whose intense pain has been relieved by sugar pills. Others have had remarkable improvement after being given a placebo for disabling depression

And perhaps nature also has a built-in placebo dynamic by which a person can relieve most or all of his deepest anxieties and fears about his existence, by being told that just by affirming that he possesses the ability to overcome these worries, (with or without religious belief), the ability will become actual. Perhaps the placebo effect underlies the resulting mystical ecstasy; and the physical experience of ecstasy might be due to a release of dopamine to the brain.

The human psyche has the apparent ability to decide that it does not have to worry about any material event; this is called "deliverance." If the decision is made with the right finesse, it does indeed result in an undauntable sense of deliverance, accompanied by a benign attitude toward all other beings.

As you may have guessed, the question of whether or not spiritual ecstasy is merely a placebo is of no consequence to the pragmatic apophatic mystic. She does not care why she has fallen in love with every-thing.

^^^

After I've written a fairly good book about apophatic mysticism, I might think I have attained a reliable grasp of mystical practice. I might even have begun to think that I have solved all of life's basic existential dilemmas. Those tacit assumptions will be a good sign that I have taken a bad turn. Consummate mastery is no more than an endearing myth. In the end, understanding and efficiency become fruitless. Ignorance, ineptitude, fear, and doubt are the reliable deliverers to ecstasy. Love is the art of the artless.

I don't know where I came from, or what I am, or what my value is, if any. I do know that my provisional aim here is to enjoy myself. A sense of the fragility of my existence brings me the realization of unconditional love, and the ecstasy obtained with that love. I have yet to find anything else more enjoyable.

I have found nothing more endurably erotic than naked presence, freedom from any obligation to be anywhere else but *now*, right here where I meet each one of you. This moment is where I find my greatest pleasure, happily in love with everything.

Resources

Books:

Mystical Languages of Unsaying, Michael A. Sells, The University of Chicago Press, 1994.

The Soul as Virgin Wife, Amy Hollywood, University of Notre Dame Press, 1995.

The Wisdom Of No Escape, Pema Chödrön, Shambhala, 1991.

The Essential Rumi, Translation by Coleman Barks with John Moyne, A. J. Arberry, and Reynold Nicholson, HarperCollins, 1995.

The Varieties of Religious Experience, William James, New American Library, 1958.

Chuang-Tzu, The Inner Chapters, A.C. Graham, Unwin Paperbacks, 1981.

Zohar: The Book of Splendor, Gershom Scholem, Schocken Books, 1963.

Yoga: Immortality and Freedom, Mircea Eliade, Princeton University Press, 1958.

Original Tao, Harold Roth, Columbia Press, 1999.

The Tao of the Tao Te Ching, Michael LaFargue, State University of New York Press, 1992.

Web sites:

The Mystical Site:
http://www.mysticism.nl/

Integral mysticism (discussion):
http://integralmysticism.getforum.org/board/index.php

Mysticism (Belief Net):
http://community.beliefnet.com/forums/forumdisplay
.php?f=348

William James: THE VARIETIES OF RELIGIOUS
EXPERIENCE:
http://xroads.virginia.edu/~HYPER/WJAMES/cover.
html

Apophatic Mysticism:
http://www.apophaticmysticism.com/

Questions for the author?

You can find me by using "search" on the Internet
community: www.facebook.com

Or: "apophatic mysticism" on facebook.com—
http://www.facebook.com/home.php?ref=logo#/group
.php?gid=124690415370

Photograph by Michael Sohigian

From a mystical point of view, I think there is a lot to be said for ignoring personal history, and yet there is also a little to be said in favor of giving a brief résumé. I've worked as a day-laborer in Queens, New York; a brakeman on the Norfolk and Western Railroad; a farmhand near Dundee, Ohio; a high school teacher in Tamale, Ghana; a forward artillery observer in Khe Sanh, Vietnam; a psychiatric nurse in Los Angeles; a plumber's assistant in the World Bank Building; and a busboy in Athens, Ohio. I've practiced mystical cultivation for a number of years, and although I am pretty good at it, I have only scratched the surface. Yet, despite being at this modest level, I have no problem appreciating what it is that causes me to love you and every other being.

Postscript: The all-embracing

It is my experience that the ability to be all-embracing, (what the classical daoists called "rong"), is spontaneously generated when a person realizes her own total and immutable innocence. In this realization one senses that there is no fundamental sin, and that there never has been any. Apparently everything has been made precisely to work as it could best be done, by whatever power created this world of experience that surrounds us: the things of this world are made so that they work well for us at times, and also functionally designed such that they fail miserably for us at other times. Gain and loss are the animators of this world. Without gain and loss nothing could move.

Despite what some folks think, the realization of immutable innocence does not entail antinomianism (doing absolutely anything one can and desires to do). This is because love, the most self-beneficial thing I can engage in, requires a trusting intimacy. I cannot get close to you if I am only focused on meeting my own self-limiting desires. What is in my interest is of a much wider scope than what I am able to imagine.

Immutable innocence means that whatever I do and have done, no matter whether it has caused healing or injury to others, I sense that it was the best I was capable of doing at the time, given my scant understanding of what I thought was in my best interest at the time. When I have gained enough wisdom, I will realize that what is most often in your best self-interest is also in my best self-interest.

If we realize our immutable innocence, if we love ourselves as unconditionally as we are able, our love will flood forth from our hearts effortlessly, saturating each of the moments in which we encounter another being. Loving ourselves unconditionally allows us to love all others unconditionally. That does not mean I will not hurt you if I think that you are needlessly hurting someone else. It does mean that I will love you no matter what you do.

"Your preciousness lies in your essence; it cannot be lost by anything that happens." Zhuangzi Chapter 21

When I understand that, I will be free. At that moment there will be no one who I will not love.